A MALLAIG BOYHOOD

John Alexander MacKenzie

ISIS
LARGE PRINT
Oxford

First published in Great Britain 1996
by
Tuckwell Press

Published in Large Print 2008 by ISIS Publishing Ltd.,
7 Centremead, Osney Mead, Oxford OX2 0ES
by arrangement with
Birlinn Limited

British Library Cataloguing in Publication Data
MacKenzie, John Alexander
    A Mallaig boyhood. – Large print ed.
    (Isis reminiscence series)
    1. MacKenzie, John Alexander – Childhood and
    youth
    2. Large type books
    3. Mallaig (Scotland) – Social life and customs
    – 20th century
    4. Mallaig (Scotland) – Biography
    I. Title
    941.1'56083'092

ISBN 978–0–7531–9472–0 (hb)
ISBN 978–0–7531–9473–7 (pb)

Printed and bound in Great Britain by
T. J. International Ltd., Padstow, Cornwall

Contents

Preface

This book is not the work of a historian, nor yet of an author; it is merely the story as I recall it of what happened to me and what I did as a child between the ages of ten to fourteen, during the final years before my family left Mallaig.

Over sixty years have passed since I was that child. Memory and indeed forgetfulness may have altered minor details, but the basic story is a combination of comedy, tenderness, fear and anguish; and above all a look at the transitional period between childhood and youth.

I am indebted to my wife and both of my children and their respective wife and husband for their help and the continual encouragement they have given me. Without their assistance and interest, this book would never have been written.

"When we look back and forgetfully remember
What we were like in our work and play . . ."

J.A. MacKenzie
Glenelg
Monmouth

CHAPTER
ONE

Earliest Days

I enjoyed a wonderful childhood, and by that I mean a childhood full of wonder and pleasure with very few disappointments.

I was the youngest of seven children, having three brothers and three sisters, and on youthful reflection I was quite sure that I must have been loved by my parents, but I was often not wanted, especially by my brothers and sisters.

My brothers had their own interests and pursuits and tended to ignore me; my sisters, on the other hand, had the nigh-on impossible task of having to look after me when we were outdoors, and, in the normal family manner, the pecking order decreed that the youngest of my three sisters ended up with the responsibility of my welfare.

This she naturally resented, as it meant that she could not run and play games with the rest of the girls because I could not run very fast, and if she ran on and left me I remember being very adept at bawling my head off. This resulted in the game being stopped and my custodian well and truly lectured for not carrying out her duty and looking after me.

Poor Cathie was only four years older than me, and I think I looked upon her as my nanny and teacher, and even, at times, my confidante.

I was born just after the end of the First World War, so of course I have no recollection of that event, but even ten years after the cessation of hostilities most of my peers were able to sport military or naval souvenirs brought back by their fathers.

There were badges, buckles, buttons, belts, rounds of rifle ammunition (no doubt rendered harmless, but we had no way of knowing that) — and ugly-looking jack-knives were equally prized.

The possession of similar treasures was denied to me as my father held a responsible position on the railway during the war and thus was in a reserved occupation and unable to enlist. The only military accoutrement he possessed was a triangular brass lapel badge embossed with the words "ON WAR SERVICE".

This was the only wartime momento he had and it was shown to me when I was called up to enlist in the army in 1939 prior to World War II.

This type of badge was prominently displayed by men who were suitable for military service but had not volunteered to join the forces.

The wearer of the badge was immune from accusations of cowardice, and so did not suffer the indignity of being given the white feather, as was the practice during World War I.

When I returned home at the end of World War II, I showed some interest in it and my father gave it to me. I have now given it to my son, and I am sure that in turn he will pass it on to his son.

CHAPTER
TWO

My Father

Having climbed up the twenty steps to our house and arrived at the landing on the top of the stairs, further progress was barred by the house door. Very prominently displayed on the door was a highly-polished brass plate bearing, in bold capital letters, the inscription:

ALEX^R MACKENZIE

This was my father, a person with whom I was acquainted, but whom I never got to know intimately.

He came from Skye and was of crofter stock. Oddly enough I don't think he ever went back to Skye, although the ferry boat crossed over at least twice a day.

Skye folk were not very well liked in the village; like the Morar boys who attended our school, all the Skye folk appeared to be very clannish and spoke only Gaelic.

My father was bilingual — Gaelic was his first language. He was one of the greatest introverts that I have ever met, and I don't think his Skye background was ever noticed. Skye folk were reputed to be lazy but resourceful, quite handy at doing jobs around the house, but my father was none of these things. I'm sure if you asked him what D.I.Y. represented, he would have replied: "Don't Involve Yourself"!

He took no part in our upbringing — he was more than content with his railway, his fishing and the garden which he made up on the line-side. And, of course, he had his hens. These pursuits, coupled with his pipe and bogey roll tobacco, made him a contented man. The *Daily Record* and the *Oban Times* on Fridays were augmented occasionally by his serious reading material: the Gaelic Bible.

We had about a dozen hens, which were looked after very well, and on many days I would be sent to the shop for half a stone (7 lbs.) of mixed grain or Indian corn and, of course, a packet of Karswood Spice. The latter was added to the household leftovers and, with potato peelings, made up the daily hot mash.

We always had plenty of eggs — even if sometimes the leftovers were mainly kipper skins and bones which, of course, promoted flavour.

Breakfast

My father invariably got up first and attended to his own breakfast. Sometimes I would waken and join him in the living room to watch his preparations. Out came the tin saucepan, known as "the wee tin pan", cold water was added and the egg was put in. This was what he always had for breakfast when he was alone.

The ashes in the grate were raked over, the oven door was opened, and out came the dried sticks, which were part of a railway sleeper and heavily creosoted. A couple of pages of the *Daily Record* were crumpled up and put in the fireplace, the sticks were added, and the wee pan was precariously balanced on top. When the match was applied the fire burnt furiously.

I was pushed to one side but I could see that within seconds the water in the pan was bubbling merrily. A couple of minutes later the pan was put on the fender, and the egg was taken out, after being chased round the pan with a teaspoon until captured.

The tea-caddy was now taken from the mantelpiece, a spoonful of tea put in the wee pan and the brew allowed to simmer while a slice of bread was buttered. The spoon in the tea-caddie was special; it looked like a miniature shovel and had the crest of Fort William on the handle.

At this stage my father sat down at the table and, using the spoon which had chased the egg around the pan, ladled two spoonfuls of sugar into his cup. Now what surprised me then was that no sugar stuck to the spoon, whereas when I once did this at tea-time I was berated for wetting the sugar in the bowl. Of course my spoon was wet and the sugar stuck to it, but my father's spoon had completely dried, having just come out of the boiling water. My father now used it to stir the tea in the cup and, when it had been given a good lick, it was used to assault the egg. At this stage he looked at me and told me to go back to bed — it was as if he saw me for the first time, or that he had just realised that I was one of his children.

On Sunday mornings breakfast always started with porridge. My father had an odd way of eating his: his porridge was put on a soup plate and was accompanied by a separate bowl of milk. He half-filled a tablespoon with the well-salted cereal, poured the milk on to the spoon to overflowing, and transferred it to his mouth. I have never seen the arrangement since. We, of course, poured the milk on to our plate in the usual orthodox fashion.

Grooming

My father polished his own boots every night ready for the next morning, and every other night he had a shaving session. The newspaper was put on the American-cloth-covered living room table, he assembled all the usual tackle: hot water in a handleless cup, a shaving brush and a bar of soap. The looking-glass was found and propped up on two or three books to give the correct angle, the cut-throat razor was taken from its cardboard container and taken over to the leather strop which always hung on the knob of the press door. Stropping the razor took several minutes and then it was returned, open, to the table.

My father then carefully positioned a chair and sat down: a signal for silence and lack of movement. The brush was soaped, dipped in hot water, and the shaving began. After each rasp the razor was wiped in a sheet of newspaper held in position on the table by a couple of books. From start to finish the operation took at least half an hour. His last task was to wind up the wall clock, and then it was off to bed for everyone.

Office work

My father's office was a single-storey, purpose-made building sited almost mid-way between the signal-box and our house. Fortunately, the door was at the back so by walking along the railway line I could nip into the signal-box undetected.

A male clerk attended my father's office four days a week. I should have said four half days, as he came from Fort William, arriving at Mallaig on the 12.10 train and going back on the 4.30p.m. I was not encouraged to visit the office, but sometimes I had to go and give my father a message or a cup of tea and, if the clerk was not present, I was allowed to stay.

I was impressed by the book press — turning the upper handle the platen on the top slowly came down and squeezed the book or papers placed on the mating platen underneath, and I had good fun putting my hand on to the book and daringly screwing down the top until my hand was held captive.

The next point of interest was the desk. This took up one side of the buildings and underneath there were several drawers complete with brass handles. On the sloping flat surface above there were four refillable inkwells, just like school ones, but best of all was the wooden box full of pen nibs, hundreds of them, all shining and golden, and all different. On one side of the box was the legend:

> *They come as a boon and a blessing to men,*
> *The Pickwick, the Owl and the Waverley pen.*

On the other side of the box was inscribed:

> *Made by MacNiven and Cameron Ltd.,*
> *Waverley Works, Edinburgh.*

Apart from the railway, my father's greatest pleasure was fishing. From a promontory almost opposite our house he would cast his line into the incoming tide. The line was secured to the top of his long bamboo rod and the only bait he would use was mussel. When he opened up the shell the contents were sucked into his mouth, freeing both his hands, and the mussel was transferred to the hook and firmly tied on with a piece of cotton thread. I asked him why he didn't use a herring as bait, but he told me he wanted to catch only Jerusalem haddies, which were red in colour, or a blue fish, which he called sea soo. I think this was sea bream or sea bass. Any other fish that he caught, such as cod, haddock or the very common saithe, were always thrown back into the sea.

The only other recreation my father had was his garden, where he grew potatoes, planted always on a bed of seaweed which he collected from the seashore. He always seemed to have a good crop and, even now, I nostalgically remember the taste of the newly-dug

Golden Wonders — boiled, dipped into some butter and sprinkled with salt.

My father's police experiences

In his younger days my father had been a policeman in Glasgow, and when I was very much older I questioned him about his police experiences. It seems that he spent the first few weeks getting to know the feel of the uniform, looking at a very large map of the city, and acting as escort helping to take the prisoners to the cells.

Two of his anecdotes interested me. Firstly, anyone taken into custody was required to empty his pockets; if no money was found he was charged with vagrancy and having no visible means of support. This charge meant that he was incarcerated to await trial by the stipendiary magistrate first thing the next morning. Conviction carried an automatic sentence of 72 hours' imprisonment. However, the police had no power to strip-search the offender and the real crafty ones had a shilling sewn into the lining of their trousers. The defendant would produce it in the morning court, stating that he had not been properly searched or, if the desk sergeant had offended him, he would swear blind that the sergeant had given it to him. In any case the charge was dismissed and he was given free bed and breakfast.

The next interesting thing was that anybody taken to jail suspected of having taken too much to drink was expected to eat a slice of bread and cheese reasonably quickly and, if he was able to do this, he was released with a caution; if not (and I remember my father saying "Some of them didn't know where their mouth was") my father and another probationer were required to drag, carry or convey the failure off to the cells. Any bread or cheese left over after the pubs had shut was dished out to the more sober citizens in the cells. In Glasgow being drunk was not, in itself, a police offence and, providing the whisky devotee was reasonably civil, he was taken to the door of his home by the police. Drunkenness only became an offence if it was accompanied by disorderly behaviour; that is, behaviour likely to cause discomfort to others, or generally being a nuisance.

At this stage in my father's police career he was quite happy, though when he went home after his shift (I think he stayed with his brother) he was obliged to change into ordinary clothes, as it was too dangerous for a policeman to be seen alone. Even today, I am told, this arrangement is observed and the Glasgow police never go on the streets unaccompanied. When my father's induction period of four weeks had passed, he was required to accompany an experienced policeman on patrol duty.

He did not go into any detail about this but it was obviously too much for him and he quit the force and was able to get a job on the Railway, stationed at Fort William, where he met and married my mother. At the turn of the century the Mallaig line was opened and he was promoted from foreman in Fort William to inspector at Mallaig.

The reason I questioned him about his service in the police force was that I knew him as a very gentle, kindly and considerate person, and the idea of him as a policeman in Glasgow was as ludicrous as suggesting to me that he had volunteered to bell the cat. I could see him only as being in the unenviable position of the mouse that had to catch the cat.

CHAPTER
THREE

My Mother

My maternal grandfather was a stonemason and also had a croft just outside Fort William. Both grandparents had died before I was born and consequently I have very little knowledge of my mother's family and background.

My father was the nominal head of the family, but Mother was the boss in all matters and, if Father was an introvert, Mother certainly made up for his social deficiencies. She was a tall, well-proportioned woman who carried herself in an almost regal manner. She knew everyone in the village and she was justly respected for her abilities.

Nursing skills

My mother had been a nurse in Belford Hospital, Fort William, and her medical knowledge was gladly shared with anyone unwilling or financially unable to seek the help of the doctor. At home our medical chest contained everything necessary for a long and healthy life. We were dosed with Scott's Emulsion, Radio Malt, and little packets of Askit or Seidlitz Powders. For scratches and bruises we had (at my father's instigation) Holloway's Ointment.

Temperament

We were all somewhat in awe of my mother; she had an ungovernable temper which she could retain at high pitch for a day at the very least. Heaven help anyone who tried to placate her when she was in one of her moods. She took offence very easily: offence which was rarely intended and often imagined.

Although I was very careful and tried not to say or do anything controversial to get her dander up, sometimes she would take offence and very angrily shout, "If you don't get out, I will take my feet to you." Now, I was never very sure what she meant by this, but running down the stairs two at a time was not conducive to further thought.

I would stay out till my father came home, hoping that by then she would have simmered down, and knowing that she could not hit me while relating my misdemeanours to my father, who patiently listened and did nothing about it. He, in turn, was abused for his indifference, but this was fine as the heat was taken off me and transferred to him.

Generosity

For all my mother's faults and failings, her greatest virtue must have been her generosity. She was prepared to give her last penny to the needy, and to me she epitomised Highland hospitality. No one ever left our house hungry or empty-handed. During the summer months tinkers came round the door asking for milk or clothes for the bairns. Even they were warmly welcomed and seated on the steps outside to be given tea and a "piece" and, of course, any clothes that my sisters had worn out or discarded.

Similarly, tramps abounded. I recall one old man playing the pipes, dressed in tartan trews and with a Stewart tartan plaid over his shoulder. He played "The Flowers of the Forest" and "Scotland the Brave", at least that was what he told my mother when she asked him what the tune was, and I know she gave him some money, which, no doubt, he spent at the local pub. I remember another tramp who rattled two spoons about his body while singing a song. I don't remember much about the song and have never heard it since; perhaps he made it up. What I remember was:

Follow me, follow me, all the bairns follow me;
Jag me wi' preens, tormenting me sorely.

Reading the tea leaves

Nothing pleased my mother more than having a ceilidh with one or two of the neighbours. Her speciality was reading the tea leaves of their "cupachan". She was reputed to excel at this skill and her company was sought by most of the tenants of the Railway Buildings and beyond.

Most days I would come home from school to find the house empty, and I would make myself a piece and go back out to play. Occasionally she would find me and explain that she was having a "wee blether" with Lexie, Maggie Ann or Flora, but she really wanted me to run down to the shop and get something for my father's dinner. The train would be in in half an hour or so, so I was instructed to hurry.

The messages

When going for messages we always had to have the book. We had two books: one for the grocer and the other for the butcher. Whatever we bought was written in the book and into the shopkeeper's book on the counter. The bill was settled every two weeks, as all railwaymen were paid fortnightly. If I was lucky enough to pay the bill, the grocer gave me a poke of sweets, which I shared with no-one at home, as they never shared with me if they had been to pay on previous occasions.

The SWRI

No social event took place in the village without my mother's knowledge and consent: in fact she originated all the concerts and the Scottish Women's Rural Institute outings. In the village any female brave enough to sport the SWRI badge was deemed to be a Scottish Woman Running Idle. As there was so much shifting of Railway folk the Rural's fortunes rose and

16

fell, and the replacement railwayman's wife was visited and welcomed by my mother, who pointed out all the advantages of membership of this august body.

Knitting

Mother always had her knitting on the go, either socks or jerseys, and I was often caught and made to help unwind the hanks of wool while she rewound it into a ball. It was a case of arms forward, palms facing each other, thumbs pointing to the ceiling, and this pose was often held for an hour and a half. Heaven help me if I fidgeted.

Duncan made some sort of contraption mounted between the jambs of the kitchen door to do this job, but it obviously was not as good as I was and did not last very long. Thank goodness I was not required to assist in the making of the clootie rugs.

Culinary skills

Mother's culinary ability was somewhat limited, and as a result our menu was restricted. Her favourite meal was mince, and going to the butcher's was a job I avoided if at all possible, mainly because of the instructions which I had from her: "Here's the bread, here's the book, and tell him you want a pound and a half of stewing steak. Watch him cut the slices and give him the bread and tell him it has to be minced up".

The bread was usually the crusts of the loaf in use at home, something normally given to the hens. I had to

17

watch the butcher wind it through his mincer, and check that the steak was not put in until I could see the bread crumbs coming out. After the steak had been minced I had to give him the other crust and wait and see that he did not stop winding until the bread appeared. This was apparently necessary to ensure that you were given only your steak and not somebody else's rubbish which had been left in the machine; at least this was Mother's contention and Mother was always right.

Strangely enough, the butcher accepted this arrangement as normal, but I would hang around outside the shop, wait till it was empty and go in hoping that no one would come in and watch the performance.

Normally the mince was dished out in the usual manner with carrot, turnip or swede, and onions, but as a diversion we sometimes had mince patties. These were most desirable and were made of mince, rolled out and covered in flour, divided into rounds like fairy cakes. They were put on to a well-greased frying-pan, and allowed to simmer over the fire.

When they were done they were kept warm in the oven and the stovies were put into the pan. Stovies were made of cooked potato and chopped onion, rolled out like patties and, when crisped up in the drained frying pan, they made a meal fit for a king.

Another favourite was sausage and tatties. Sausage came in two kinds: links or sliced. We always had sliced, and when cooked with rounds of black pudding, this made a delicious meal.

Fish, of course, was the staple diet: kippers, herring and white fish, which Roddy took home from the pier

— usually flounders or skate wings, which were always very nice but served to excess. The fish which my father caught were special. They were unusual because of the colour, and before my father took them into the house he scraped off all the scales. I do not know why, but this seemed to be part of the preparation prior to boiling in salt water. To me these fish did not taste very different from any others — fish was fish as far as I was concerned — but my father considered them a treat and we were expected to show appreciation at being allowed to share this choice fare.

On reflection, we seemed to use a lot of bread; we bought it in units of four loaves. The bread came from Glasgow and was packed in very large wicker hampers marked Beattie's Bread. There were two types of bread: plain or pan. We always had plain, which came ready-wrapped in waxed paper. A good many hampers were shipped out to the Hebrides by MacBrayne's passenger boats and the wrapping might have been necessary to preserve the freshness.

Mutton soup

We never had pudding, but my mother's soup was a speciality. No-one could make soup as she did, and while we all had two platefuls each time, she did not make it very often, but it was a great favourite and always delicious. It was made from mutton stock, and we then ate the mutton itself from the soup plate and helped ourselves to the potatoes and vegetables, which were on the table in individual ashets. I don't remember any gravy, but butter was always to hand as an alternative. Before we ate my father always said grace: hand on brow, some words mumbled in Gaelic. As his hand left his forehead we all said "Amen".

Anonymous gift

The reason the soup was so incredibly good makes an interesting story. The gigot of mutton from which it was made was an anonymous gift. It was found at the foot of the stairs just inside the front door, neatly wrapped in paper. When it was discovered and brought upstairs my mother would send me to the shop for six pennyworth of carrot and turnip before I went to school. Years later I learned the whole story.

It seemed that a sheep had broken through the railway fence and been hit by the train. Provided it was not a passenger train it would stop and the sheep would be pulled on to the footplate of the locomotive where, if it had not been killed, it was quickly dispatched and allowed to bleed. The blood was hosed off while the train continued on its way.

On the return of the locomotive to the Mallaig engine shed the sheep was skinned and cut up into joints; one hind leg was reserved for my father, the other rear gigot was for the engine driver, the fore legs for the fireman and the guard. The remainder of the carcass was distributed among the rest of the locomotive staff and all the evidence, including the skin, was consigned to the fire on the locomotive.

My father was chosen as a recipient for two reasons: firstly it showed tremendous regard for my parents, and secondly it told him that the fence had been breached. I was puzzled when Mother opened up the parcel and Father asked her if she had got the letter.

Years later I learned that the letter in the package was a page torn out of the local train timetable, with a line drawn in pencil, either between two stations or under the name of one station. This told my father where the fence was damaged.

As fences were part of his responsibility, he was able to dispatch one of his two fencers to carry out the necessary repairs without having the trouble of looking for the damage along forty miles of track. My father had about twenty men under his command in Mallaig and, in addition to the normal ten men responsible for track maintenance, he had the black-smith and striker, two painters, two fencers, two joiners and a motley gang of stonemasons. There were, in addition, the six length men who, with their wives and families, lived along the railway track, and whom I will mention later when I tell of how Alistair delivered illicit coal and was rewarded with tattie scones.

21

CHAPTER
FOUR

Duncan

Our family was the second largest in the Railway Buildings — the MacKays had eight children, and although they only had one bedroom in their house they still managed to find room to keep a lodger. It was suggested that they all slept in hammocks hanging from hooks in the two bed recesses.

As far as I remember, although I was one of seven children, it seemed to me that we had more than enough room, and I can recall being put to bed in the wee room, but always put at the bottom of the bed. Alistair, the eldest, was always on night shift, so Roddie and Duncan shared the top of the bed. Alistair got into bed when we got out, and I think that the three girls slept in a somewhat similar fashion in the big room. My father and mother slept in the bed recess, which meant that they had to be last going to bed and first to get up.

Family groupings

Perhaps at this stage I should try to explain some details about the family. As a unit we were made up of three distinct groups, splinter groups in fact. The two eldest boys were always at loggerheads, either with each other or while being bullied by my three sisters, who appeared to get on fairly well together. Duncan and I made up the last group; while we rarely agreed with one another, we had to present a united front when we were attacked by either or both of the other groups.

Each group was a self-contained unit, and little outside help was given or asked for. I knew I belonged to the family but was never a part of it. I could not get advice from Duncan except if he was in a good mood, or his answer showed off his superior knowledge, and at the same time emphasised my lack of knowledge. He had a very quick temper, and as he was bigger and older than me I had to bite my tongue very often.

In modern parlance, Duncan was a "loner". He preferred not to share any glory resulting from his usually futile experiments. He was continually fiddling about with bits and pieces in our shed and, of course, I was rarely admitted. Most of my associations with him ended to my disadvantage, and while I realised this, I always fell for his charms when called upon to render some help.

Ice cream

Duncan used to help make the ice cream for the Refreshment Rooms by the Station. He and a partner had to wind the handle of the ice-cream machine until the contents had solidified. On one occasion it appeared that his partner was sick and would I help him just this once until his mate was able to return? I wasn't very keen on the idea, but the lure of the sixpence reward and the opportunity of being allowed to lick out the ice cream from the paddles was too much for me, so I agreed to help out, just this once.

We set off bright and early the very next morning, and found the manager setting up the equipment. There was a fairly large drum inside which was a second, much smaller drum. The space between was filled with ice chippings and, for some reason which I didn't understand, coarse salt was shovelled on top.

The ice-cream mixture was poured from a pail into the inner drum, the paddles were put into position, a lid was positioned with the paddle spindle on top, the gearing and handles were fitted and the whole top assembly was bolted together. Now it was our turn: all we had to do was to wind the handle until it was too tight to turn, by which time the ice cream would have set. Duncan took the first turn at the handle winding but as the contraption was inclined to wobble about I had to sit on the top in an effort to limit its perambulations.

Duncan gave up after a short time; now it was my turn on the handle. I was encouraged by being told how good I was at this, and as he was heavier than I was he would stay sitting on top while I turned the handle. When I could turn it no more Duncan had a short go and soon went off to find the man to tell him it was ready. The contraption was dismantled and the inner drum removed after the ice cream sticking to the paddles had been scraped off. While the inner container was carried into the building, the paddles were left for me to lick.

There was precious little left to lick but I still had the sixpence to look forward to: I would buy a tuppenny slider and have it all to myself. Ice cream was dispensed in pokey hats (cones) at a ha'penny and sliders (wafers) could be had for a penny for a small one and tuppence for a large. I had never had a large slider but I was determined to buy one as soon as I received the promised reward for my Herculean efforts.

I waited some little time for Duncan to come back — he had helped to carry the ice-cream drum into the shop — but in despair I went into the shop, only to find him and the manager sitting at a table, obviously enjoying a huge plateful of our newly-created product.

I went off home very downcast, feeling very cheated; after all, I had done most of the work. When I met up with Duncan again I demanded my sixpence, only to be told that he had been given a shilling and I would have to wait till he had change. I never did see my share of the earnings; instead I was to be privileged to join in the latest money-making scheme.

We were to make our own ice cream and my sixpence would help to buy some of the necessary ingredients. After all, he told me, ice cream was only frozen Cremola custard powder, and he would make a mixing unit to beat it all up.

Sure enough he did make a contraption: the outside drum was half a herring barrel, the inner drum an enamel pail, with the rotating mechanism adapted from bicycle parts. The top of this was a chain-driven gear wheel complete with pedal, which was the handle for driving the wooden paddles. When I tried it, it seemed to work all right, although it did wobble about a bit. Duncan assured me that this was because it was empty, and he would sort it out by adding a bottom bearing, a piece of wood with a central hole, wedged in the bottom of the pail.

So far I had taken no active part in this business enterprise, but my turn had now come. I was to get the custard powder (no money provided from petty cash), a saucepan and at least one egg. Duncan, in the meantime, was reconditioning a Valor Beatrice paraffin stove which he had previously rescued from the spring tide waves. It had two wicks, but the mechanism for raising or lowering them had been broken off, and in spite of this and the leaking tank it would be as good as new when serviced by the expert.

The big day arrived and the stove was lit (we had access to plenty of rape oil), the saucepan was put on top, half-filled with water, and I was sent off to get the Cremola. The custard powder, the egg and a little water were all mixed up in a bowl borrowed from home, and I must admit I was very surprised at how good it looked.

The mixture was poured into the saucepan and about a pint of water was added before it was put on the stove. When it had almost reached boiling point, Duncan remembered that sugar had to be added at this stage, so I had to run home and collect about a pound from the sugar bag at home. In our house sugar was bought in units of seven pounds, so my pilferage was not noticed. When the sugar had been added, the mixture was allowed to simmer for quite a long time and then poured into the enamelled pail to cool until the next day.

The following day Duncan was up bright and early and when we met up at school time he told me that we had to double up the quantity, as the mixture only just reached the paddles. I suggested more water, but no, the mixture had to be just right, and so after school I "borrowed" the grocery book and got more Cremola and two pounds of sugar.

Duncan, meanwhile, had another egg, and he proceeded with his usually culinary skill to repeat yesterday's efforts. On day three I was given the hen's pail and told to get the ice and the salt.

Mallaig boasted an ice factory, and barrels of ice were often taken by lorry to the pier, so it was a simple matter to fill the pail with the overspill lying on the bed of the Fiat or the Ford. Salt, too, was easily had as it was used to pickle the barrels of herring.

Duncan was waiting for me with all the machinery ready, but as usual there was yet one more hurdle to overcome: the lumps of ice were too big to go between the two containers. I was amazed how difficult it was to break the ice into usable size; I had always looked on ice as a very brittle substance, but it took all my efforts and my father's hatchet to break up enough for our use. We managed it in the end and with great pleasure began the winding process.

We took it in turns and everything seemed to go according to plan. The process should have taken about half an hour, but in our eagerness we had not allowed the standing time of about an hour to allow the chill to get through to the mixture, and consequently we had to wind it all up for a much longer period. According to the expert, this was all to the good as it would make for a much smoother ice cream.

The moment of truth arrived at last. The inner container was removed and together we carried it into the shed and hurriedly opened it up. It looked odd to me: it was perfectly white to look at and on closer examination it was seen to consist of ice crystals.

The drum was inverted and bumped on to the floor, but although there was no ice cream, some ice did come out. We dug through the ice to find the eagerly desired product, and eventually found it, as hard as well-seasoned concrete. Only with the aid of a claw-hammer were we able to get any out at all. Duncan heated up some water and, having poured it into the drum, he extracted the culmination of our efforts: frozen custard, eatable only when chopped up with the claw-hammer.

According to the Head Cook the eggs were put in to prevent separation, but for some reason the mixture was not stabilised properly. It would be better next time. There would be no next time for me!

I think I enjoyed sucking the ice crystals as much as chewing through the "ice cream". Actually it tasted quite good; at least it was sweet, but a little went a long way, as when the mouth became numbed the taste disappeared and so the mixture was eventually poured away behind the shed some two or three days later.

So much for our combined business expertise! The two scallop shells that I had collected to act as plates for my anticipated orgy I was obliged to dump unused, but I did stand them up tent-fashion by the shed door as a reminder of what might have been.

Duncan was very down in the dumps, really crestfallen. It was not so much the fact that his ice-cream efforts had been abortive, but that I had witnessed his failure. He tried to excuse his lack of success by telling me that we should have used milk and not water, and that one of the wooden paddles had popped out as we dumped the mixture simply because the fence wire that had been used to secure it to the central spindle had broken. He qualified this by saying that the other paddle had not come adrift, proving that it was a faulty piece of wire. I am now quite certain that no mixing process ever took place and that the contents of the inner container remained emulsified.

However, this was my big chance. Duncan was very depressed and even went to the bother of confiding in me in an effort to justify his lack of success.

"Where is my sixpence?" I demanded, "Can I have it now?" His reply was fairly typical: he had spent a lot of money getting all the materials for the store and making up the machine, and he had no money. However, he would let me have one of his bottles of sugarallie water to make up for it.

He had boasted in the past how delicious this elixir was. It was made up of liquorice strap chopped up and pushed into a water-filled lemonade bottle with a little sugar. The screw top was fitted and the bottle was kept

29

in the dark for about a week. It was taken out from under the bed every day and given a good shake before being replaced.

After about a week it was examined and I noticed that it was now capped with a head of froth. It was pronounced fit to be tasted and Duncan poured some out into a cup. It was as dark as black boot polish and the vile smell was equalled by its taste. I was obliged to have several tastings later and, although I told him I quite liked it, most of it ended up down the toilet pan. Duncan was pleased I liked it, as he explained that some folk didn't get the taste right away!

The sugarallie water incident may have provided an amusing interlude, but the story of the ice-cream making is not yet finished.

Perks

It was the usual practice for boys of Duncan's age to await the arrival of the first passenger train at about 12.30. The reason for this was that the passengers alighting and sailing on to the Hebrides would leave their newspapers in the compartment and, of course, these were eagerly snatched up and sold at half price.

This train also provided the influx of the daily papers from Glasgow. There were no corridors in the trains in those days and the boys had to run alongside the carriages and entered the compartment only when they saw something of value. This was normally only newspapers but I believe other forgotten articles were sometimes to be found. At any rate, this practice got out of hand and the passenger guard who had accompanied the train from Fort William considered these finds as one of his perks and put a stop to it.

He and Duncan fell out and although Gemmell, the guard, lived only one block away, they ignored each other. As Duncan had been forced to give up this lucrative source of income, he naturally felt very bitter towards the whole Gemmell family, including Gemmell's two sons.

The sea cuckoo

It so happened that when Duncan needed to find an egg for our ice cream project, he knew that Gemmell had been assembling a setting of eggs. As he had no cockerel himself, he was dependent on others to provide a dozen eggs for his clocker (broody hen) to sit on and hatch out, and one or two of the setting wouldn't be missed.

Duncan went up to Gemmell's hen house, fearlessly risking pecking injury, and took not one egg but two to use in our second batch of Cremola mixture. It so happened that the very next day a fisher lass gave Duncan two eggs: "These will do for Alistair's tea". Duncan knew full well that we were well off for eggs and, filled with remorse, braved the clocker once more and put the eggs back underneath.

Weeks later there was great consternation in the Railway Buildings and people came from far and near to see Gemmell's chicks. In the pen provided there were ten yellow chicks and two grey ones, the latter with webbed feet. A sea cuckoo had got into the hen house, not once, but twice. This was unheard of.

"Did you see Gemmell's chickens with the webbed feet? Well, they're sea cuckoos." I don't think the mystery was ever solved and neither Duncan nor myself ever offered the solution: Gemmell's hen had hatched out two baby seagulls.

Gemmell's son Ian was in my class at school and normally answered to the nickname of Speedy; he had gained this nom-de-plume as he was a very fat lad and consequently showed little effort in any practical activity. His nickname changed overnight and he became Cuckoo Gemmell.

The St Kilda Postal Service

I must admit that I do not know what started it all off, but much later, after the ice-cream débâcle, when I assured myself that never would I ever again become a party to Duncan's schemes, I was once more in the midst of things.

It could well have been that Duncan's class had had a lesson about St Kilda; he certainly had knowledge that had been denied to me, and he certainly hadn't read about the St Kildans' method of posting a letter during the winter season when no boats were able to call.

It could well be that his interest had been triggered by the S.S. *Hebrides*, which had arrived at the big pier, awaiting coal and other materials for its trip to St Kilda.

This boat, or should I say ship, was owned by McCallum Orme and Co., of Glasgow, and the same company were the owners of the *Dunara Castle*. Mallaig was the last mainland port of call and, after her two days' stay she would set sail for the "Famous St Kilda Tour". Passengers were carried and cared for on the ship and during the summer months the excursion took place at least four or five times. It was not possible to dock and all visits ashore were by means of the ship's lifeboat.

Apparently everyone on the largest island, Hirta, stood on the jetty to greet the invaders, but as only Gaelic was used, communication was not possible and visitors could only take a quick look round the island to see the primitive conditions while awaiting the unloading.

Duncan gave me the benefit of his superior knowledge and went to some lengths to explain the postal service used during the winter months.

He explained that a sheep's bladder was blown up and tied with a piece of gristle. A piece of wood was attached to the bladder, and securely fastened to that was a bottle containing a letter. A note inside asked the finder to post the letter, which bore the name and address but no postage stamp.

Why didn't we have a shot at this, asked my brother. "You're pretty good at finding things and we could make the boat out of cork." He would make a list of all the things I was to get and he would do the building. I found the idea most exciting, and after giving it much thought I couldn't for the life of me see how I could lose out this time, so I agreed to be his partner.

The items on the list were: a slab of cork from the chest piece of a life jacket (this was the largest block of cork, measuring about 9 × 9 inches), a glass float and some lobster creel cord, well barked, as it might be in the sea for a long time.

I had some difficulty in finding a life jacket; life belts were common but not life jackets. Eventually I saw one and so, given time and the opportunity, this would start my collection.

It is difficult to stuff your jersey with a block of cork this size, and so although I knew where to find the cork, it was hard for me to find a way to deliver it to Duncan. I explained my dilemma to him and he immediately provided the solution: make up a parcel using brown paper and new string and carry it as though it was a book. I grabbed the life jacket and, hiding behind a stack of herring boxes, quickly ripped open the canvas and made up my parcel as suggested. This was a great success; nobody questioned the contents of my parcel and, when delivered, it was eagerly pounced upon and on examination was pronounced perfect. This was to be the hull of the boat.

When next I saw it it was perfectly shaped, with bow and stern and the middle of the boat exactly and expertly cut away to house the empty whisky half-bottle. That was to be the container for the letter, and I was assured that when the screw cap was tightly fitted it would be watertight. The keel was made of lead salvaged from the fog signals. My mate had made a mould in a turnip, melting the lead on his Valor stove, and producing a very presentable keel. All we needed now was the glass float. I couldn't see the need for this, but Duncan assured me that if the cork boat was broken up it would be safer if we had a glass float and, in any case, it would be found more easily when beached on some far and distant land.

I had no difficulty in getting a float; the herring nets had just been barked (preserved) and were hanging on all the fences, and even some of the rocks, to dry.

The float we encased in lobster creel net, which was ideal for attaching it to our boat. Duncan was very pleased with my latest acquisition, so much so that he would finish it all himself. The mast, sail and keel were fixed on and the parts was linked by using lobster-creel cord.

I had no part in the wording of the letter but I was permitted to read it. In neat block capitals a reward was offered to the person who returned it "to the address below". The envelope was embossed O.R.B. (On Railway Business). I wondered where he got it, but no doubt it was taken from my father's office. My father would have been furious if he had known.

I was informed that the launching would take place on the ebb tide following the next spring tide in about a week's time.

When the time came I was very impressed to see the ship with its very tall mast, canvas sail (part of a life jacket), rigging running fore and aft from the mast head and, of course, the keel, securely fastened through the boat and attached to the bottle.

The great day eventually arrived. After tea we set off for the promontory where my father went fishing. Duncan had everything ready for the launch, including my father's bamboo fishing rod to push the result of our mutual efforts out to sea.

The boat and its appendages seemed most reluctant to leave, and only with Duncan's efforts with my father's rod did it eventually leave us and set out on its journey. I was really sorry to see its departure: it looked very forlorn, bobbing about on the ebbing tide, and to me it meant discarding something very precious.

We watched it together as long as it was clearly visible, and then made our way home in the gathering darkness. I asked Duncan when we would hear where it had landed, and I was assured that with a bit of luck it would end up in Newfoundland. According to him this was due west from Mallaig. He did, however, qualify this, saying that if the currents were strong and the winds variable it might end up on Skye or, perhaps, on the south coast of Greenland, but the longer the reply took, the further the post boat would have travelled.

I waited a very long time but no reply ever came. On reflection, the boat probably ended up round the Khyber, having travelled about two sea miles. It is just possible, however, that it returned to its origins in Village Bay, Hirta. I will never know.

On leaving school Duncan got a job at the hydro-electric scheme at Morar Falls, and cycled there daily from home. When this job finished he left home and worked on other hydro schemes. He failed his army medical test at the outbreak of the war and was transferred to "work of national importance", finally ending up at Scapa Flow, where he helped build the Churchill Causeway, constructed to prevent a further raid on Britain's shipping anchored there. The causeway shut off the entry through which a German U-boat had been able to enter and sink H.M.S. *Ark Royal* with great loss of life.

Duncan married an Orcadian girl and settled down outside Kirkwall. After the war he worked for the local electricity generating company. Electricity was provided by stationary engines, just as it had been in Mallaig twenty years earlier.

CHAPTER
FIVE

Alistair and Roddy

Memories of my eldest brother, Alistair, are somewhat vague. This was understandable as he was some fifteen years older than I was and I saw so little of him: he worked a permanent night shift as an engine cleaner, with numerous other duties, such as turning the engines on the turntable, coaling the locomotives, and cleaning and oiling the external driving shafts. Every engine leaving the station was spotless, its bumpers gleaming.

Alistair's final daily task, perhaps the most important, was to wake up all the people necessary for the first train to leave at 7.30a.m. He had to tap on the window of at least six houses with his long bamboo pole, waiting for acknowledgement each time before moving on to the next house.

Well do I remember that he was our alarm clock: at about 8a.m. he would wake Duncan and me and, if we were in any way tardy, he would pull us out of bed. He was already washed and undressed and would quickly occupy the bed which we were obliged to vacate.

Alistair and Roddy seemed to smoke cigarettes incessantly and, apart from the enjoyment they derived from them, an auxiliary pleasure was the acquisition of cigarette cards. Alistair once told me he only smoked to get the cards. The bedroom fireplace was choc-a-bloc with empty Capstan packets and any overflow, including cigarettes, took up a position on the furniture. When my sisters grumbled at them and made them tidy up, a match was applied to the accumulation in the grate.

Capstan cigarettes cost the equivalent of five new pence for twenty, but of course the cigarette cards were the prized possessions. They had collected sets of locomotives, steam-and sailing-ships, sportsmen and members of the Royal Family, past and present. Later a change took place and the cards were part of a large painted picture. It was necessary to collect jigsaw pieces, and when all the pieces had been collected they were posted off to *W.D and H.O. Wills, Bristol, England* who sent back a full-size picture rolled in a cardboard tube. We had three of these pictures: *The Boyhood of Raleigh, When Did You Last See Your Father?* and *Mother and Son. The Boyhood of Raleigh* showed a young boy in knickerbockers sitting on a sea wall; an old man was standing alongside him, with his right hand raised, pointing out to sea at some sailing ships passing in the distance. *When Did You Last See Your Father?* again showed a young boy, standing by a long wooden table, being questioned by a group of soberly dressed men seated and wearing top hats. *Mother and Son* showed a mare and a foal in a field with a farmhouse in the background. The pictures were never framed but were pinned up on the bedroom wall.

The next sales incentive was "free playing cards". Each cigarette packet of ten provided one miniature playing card and, of course, there were two cards in the larger packet. The smoker was obliged to collect all 52 cards and send them off to Wills at Bristol. An arrangement was in force which allowed the smoker to write for a particular card in exchange for any two cards which were enclosed in the letter. Needless to say, the main activity during playtime was swapping with other boys in an effort to assemble a complete pack, at the instigation, of course, of our elder brother or father.

The only other activity that I remember Alistair and Roddy sharing was listening to Radio Luxembourg on the wireless set, tuned to 208 metres medium wave. This was an evening programme and consisted of the latest gramophone hits, interspersed with adverts. The reason for their avid interest was the invitation to the listener to write in for free samples of the advertised products.

Alistair seemed to be in charge of the scheme and we had razor blades, brushless shaving cream, Kolynos toothpaste, Icilma cream, Ponds vanishing cream, Amami shampoo, Horlicks tablets, little cardboard boxes of Ovaltine, and lots more, including Beecham's powders, worth a guinea a box and a cure for all ailments. I tried out the vanishing cream on my wart one night, but it didn't seem to work; the wart was still in position when I examined my hand first thing in the morning.

Any of these samples could be had for a 12d. stamp, and our family took full advantage of the *free* offers.

Because of the difference in our ages, I must have been ten and Alistair twenty-five when he married Jeannie, a fisher lass from Eyemouth. Although he continued to live in the village, our paths rarely crossed, a situation exacerbated, of course, by his unusual working hours.

I do remember that there was some anxiety about finding the couple somewhere to live. Eventually, with my mother's capable assistance, they were able to have a room in a council house with Big Agnes. This was not very satisfactory and they soon flitted to a house of their own, a large wooden hut sited behind Mrs Duncan, the baker's, shop. It was a proper wooden house divided into several rooms and a kitchen, probably the fore-runner of today's mobile home.

If I called on Jeannie with a message from my mother, I was always given a piece of cake or some biscuits and made to feel very welcome. She seemed to be a very kindly person and her house was spotless and even had a well-tended garden at the door.

Roddy

Roddy seemed to spend a lot of time away from home, following the fishing round the coast of Scotland and England. I seem to remember that he went to Grimsby and Yarmouth, but I don't really remember much about him. When he was at home he could hardly manage to eat as, with one eye on the sea, he would be waiting to dash down to the pier to greet the arrival of a fishing boat. On leaving the house he was able to tell us the name of the boat and what sort of a "shot" (catch) she had.

He was later employed by the largest fish merchants in Scotland, D.A. MacRae of Fraserburgh. He progressed from foreman to buyer and eventually became manager of the Mallaig branch.

When we left Mallaig, Roddy was foreman and married, and naturally stayed behind. It was several years after our family left that he became manager and agent.

Fish buyers were required to lodge a sum of money with the bank, and it was the duty of the agent, with the co-operation of the bank manager, to pay all debts incurred. These included all fish purchased, fuel and wage expenses, provisions and, of course, rail freight charges. All fishing boats had to have a bank clearance certificate before leaving port. Roddy was pleased to tell my father that his bond was three thousand pounds.

The firm he worked for had processing and canning facilities at Fraserburgh. The company was eventually taken over by Lever Brothers, the washing-powder and Sunlight soap empire, best known in the West Highlands for Lord Leverhulme's abortive attempts to attract industry to Lewis and Harris. Having acquired MacRaes, they opened a chain of fish shops, sadly no longer in existence, under the name of Mac Fisheries.

I don't remember Roddy's wedding; probably he was married in his wife's home town of Burnmouth. His wife Lizzie was a fisher lassie who had been at the kippering in Mallaig. She was a very upright person, but again I didn't get to know her very well, only visiting her with my mother. I think they only occupied one of the tenement houses for a short time, moving to a new council bungalow soon after. I don't remember much to-ing and fro-ing between Jeannie and Lizzie, or even between their children.

Alistair had three children and Roddy four. Sad to say, Alistair's only son is the last to carry our family's name in Mallaig.

CHAPTER
SIX

Morag, Lottie and Cathie

My eldest sister, Morag, was about eight years older than I was, and as she was a relief Post Office clerk, she spent most of her time away from home and I saw very little of her. She travelled extensively and I know that, as well as travelling to Fort William, she was directed to post offices in Argyll, Perthshire, and even to Port Ellen in Islay. I remember all this because of the postcards she sent home.

Lottie and Cathie seemed to derive great pleasure from telling me off: Did I do this? Why hadn't I done that? I suppose it was a form of bullying common in all large families. Lottie seemed to be in charge of the domestic arrangements and, particularly, the cleaning.

The stairs were pipe-clayed white and only a narrow rectangle was left bare on each step. Heaven help anyone who touched the white area, which extended up to the skirting; any infringement was easily detected, as not only did we leave a mark on the stairs, but, of course, pipe clay came off our boots and rubbed off on the mat and the transgressor was easily identified.

Running downstairs with either my mother or Duncan in hot pursuit gave me little opportunity to position my boots correctly as I galloped down two stairs at a time. However, when I eventually sneaked home, not only was I chastised by the original injured party, but of course by my sisters, complaining about the mess I had made of the stairs.

It seemed to me that either Lottie or Cathie were always on hands and knees in front of the grate, either shaking the Zebo polish on to it or polishing the already shining surface with the brush which was kept exclusively for this task, or else they were scrubbing away with emery cloth at the steel oven door handle, hinges, or the fender. All the parts gleamed to a startling brilliance excelled only by the nickel-plated handlebars of our new bike. The grate had a water tank on the opposite side to the oven; it was filled by hand through an opening at the top and, when the fire was drawing well, a limited quantity of very hot water could be had by turning the brightly polished tap. Many a tin of Brasso must have been used to polish up the taps, including the swan-necked faucet in the scullery.

Close by the fireside tap was the toaster, the only one of its kind I have ever seen. It was an open metalwork wire cage supported by interlocking strips of iron, each pivoted at one end, so that they could be opened up. With the bread in position the cage was pushed over to the bars in front of the fire and carefully guarded until the toast was ready. When not in use it was folded up and was hardly noticeable apart from the two highly polished bolts which fixed it to the grate.

I am rather vague as to how Lottie and Cathie flew the nest. I think Lottie went first to a Domestic Science college and later on Cathie went as a probationer nurse to the Victoria Hospital in Glasgow. She didn't stay there long and I think both girls finally took up positions in domestic service, leaving only Duncan and me at home as the last sore bane of my mother's life.

CHAPTER
SEVEN

Mallaig and Our House

Mallaig is a small fishing village on the north-west coast of Scotland. It is the terminus of both road and rail services and consisted of three distinct strata of population.

There was the original village, and, of course, the inhabitants were indigenous to this part of the West Highlands: crofters who were almost completely cut off from other society. As a result, very little English was spoken, or indeed understood, and the "natives" were continually ridiculed because they conversed solely in Gaelic and had little interest in or knowledge of the outside world.

The second stratum was made up of the incomers: these were the Railway people. The Railway opened in 1901 and I am sure that with the advent of the first train from Fort William the population trebled.

My parents were of this second stratum, that is, Railway people, and as such commanded a great deal of respect from the local original population.

After all, people now had titles as well as names; by that I mean Mr Gillies the Stationmaster, and my

father Mr Mackenzie the Inspector. We also had Mr
So-and-So the Guard and Mr So-and-So the Foreman
(Porter). These titles, or rather names, were revered
only if the incumbents were incomers and lived in
Railway houses. Local men who were employed by the
Railway appeared not to enjoy any such distinction.

The third stratum of Mallaig's cosmopolitan society
was made up of people involved in fishing, or its
associated industry. Most of these people came from
the north-east coast and travelled around following the
migration of the herring.

Several took up permanent residence, usually
through marriage or because they became involved in
the white fish season which followed on after the
herring season.

Our house

Our house was a Railway house, a house in a block of
four. There were four such blocks, all tenanted by
Railway employees. This made sixteen families in all,
with probably four children per household: about sixty
children in a very closely knit community. Each block
had four houses; two upstairs and two downstairs. Ours
was of the former type, and entrance was gained by
opening the outside door and walking up twenty
concrete steps.

How well I remember my first arithmetic lesson
counting those steps while holding my sister's hand:
one, two, three and finally twenty. We were now at the
stair door, which led directly into the house.

The house had two bedrooms and a living room (all with a bed recess), and a scullery with a double white china sink divided by a metal bar on which stood our wringer.

From this I had my first English lesson:

Acme Wringer Co. Ltd. Glasgow, 14 inch

This legend was boldly imprinted on the top bar just below the tension wheel, and although I could read it, I had little understanding of what it meant.

Sited on the back wall behind and at the division of the two sinks we had one brass swan-necked pipe which could be turned to discharge into either sink. There were two taps, but they were not called taps in my day; they were *faucets*.

They were marked *H* and *C* respectively and although I knew that only cold water came out of each of them, on asking my mother she told me that when the fire in the living-room was drawing well, hot water was available from the faucet marked "*H*", but only on washing days, and even then not very much hot water.

The hot water supply

On washing days, to compensate for the vagaries of the domestic hot water supply, my mother, armed with one, or sometimes even two pails, would walk down the stairs (all twenty of them) and wait at the side of the Railway track which was directly in front of the house.

When the driver of the locomotive, which was always engaged in shunting in the yard, saw her, he would drive his train of wagons to where she was, would stop, and the fireman would dismount and put the pail under the boiler discharge pipe.

The driver would then turn the valve in his cab, and when the pail of boiling water was filled, it was given to my mother. If there were two pails to be filled, the second one was carried and put over the Railway fence by the fireman to await collection.

This task completed, the train was allowed to carry on with its normal duty.

The toilet

All the Railway buildings had a flush toilet with an overhead cistern which, when activated by pulling the chain, made a dreadful noise. When this noise abated, the new sound, almost as loud, was the water in the cistern being replenished.

I was really afraid of this operation because I was unable to avail myself of this wonder, as I was too wee to reach up to the chain, and when I was somewhat older and able to stand on the toilet I was not strong enough to stimulate the monster into action.

The bath

In addition to running hot and cold water and a flush toilet we had a bath. This was in the scullery and had a wooden cover. I am not certain that the hot water was supplied by a separate boiler and fireplace sited adjacent to the bath because this equipment was very rarely used. In order to use it the cover on top had to be cleared of domestic essentials — jam jars, cups and saucers, tea pot, and the paraffin stove with the kettle on top, with the tea caddy close by.

Even after all that was cleared, the wooden cover had to be lifted off and a temporary home found for it. Is it any wonder that the bath was so little used?

When I was bathed I was made to take off everything except my shirt, sit on the wooden draining board and put my feet in the sink. I was bathed up to my waist (I had to hold up my shirt).

When this was done I was towelled dry, my trousers were put on, and I then had to turn around, dangle my legs over the draining board, and have my shirt removed and waist to face scrubbed.

Hands and teeth were washed in the washbasin in the toilet, but as that had cold water only, this task was omitted as often as possible.

Water was necessary for the locomotives, and two very large iron water tanks were positioned on the highest point of the rocks almost opposite our house. Large pipes ran to the water towers at the station. All the railway houses were supplied with water via a lead pipe which always seemed to be leaking, and I think this pipe must have been laid on the ground and covered over with a heavy layer of ballast. At any rate, when we found a leak we wiggled the pipe until a really good fountain shot up. The water came from a loch some two miles from the village, which later became a favourite angling spot for the older lads.

Electricity

Finally, not only did we have hot and cold water, a bath and a flush toilet, but wonder of wonders, we had electricity installed in our house.

When I look back on this — and I'm talking about the 1920s and '30s — it is difficult to believe that a small village like ours could boast these amenities. Perhaps I should make it clear that all sixteen houses were similarly equipped.

The electricity was used only for lighting and cost 9d. a unit. This is about 4p in the new money and I cannot recall the meter, which was situated at the foot of the stairs, ever being read, even though my father was keen to tell us not to put the light on yet as it cost 9d. a unit.

Nobody seemed to know what a unit was, but in price a unit equalled a gallon of paraffin, and we knew only too well how careful my mother was in the use of the paraffin stove on top of the bath in the scullery, especially if my father was about.

Left to herself, my mother would leave the stove on all day, or at least until the paraffin ran out. This, of course, resulted in the wick burning dry and it consequently had to be replaced frequently.

My father didn't think much of these modern gadgets. "Things are not made to last nowadays" was his observation on the tedious wick renewal operation.

CHAPTER
EIGHT

Electricity in Olden Days

As I grew older, the mystery of electricity seemed to be spoken about very frequently among the other boys in my age group or perhaps in my class at school, but no-one seemed to know where this magic power came from. We were very curious and it was even suggested that it came on the evening train.

I cannot remember when it was that someone found out that the origin of this great secret lay in a building situated between the Wee Pier (this was the fishing pier as distinct from the Big Pier which was used for shipping to the outlying islands and served by MacBrayne's boats) and the Refreshment Rooms.

When my chums and I went to have a look at this building it was silent and apparently locked up and not in use. I asked my eldest brother about it and he seemed to know. He told me (and I told my chums) that there was a big engine in there, not an engine like there was in a lorry, but a huge engine that was fixed to the floor, and when it was started up it produced electricity to light the lamps.

When I told him that we had gone to have a look at this after school but found it silent and locked up, he told me that it was only started up as it got dark, as it was only then that the lamps had to be lit, and it was stopped at bedtime when people didn't need to have the lights on.

This whole process was controlled by "Sparks", a local man whose brother was a signalman and who later became one of my best friends and from whom I learned more than I was ever taught at school.

When my chums showed scepticism about this huge engine, we agreed to meet one evening after dark to see for ourselves if what I had been told was true.

When we arrived there, there was a light above the door and on the door we could see a notice which said "NO ADMITTANCE", but best of all there was a terrific noise of an engine running or at least some machinery in motion. I was completely vindicated and preened myself on being the little hero. The mystery was at last solved!

We all went to our respective homes, but I was determined to see this amazing sight for myself. Fortune favoured me because some evenings later I was outside the building, hoping to see the moving engine; it was quite dark but the engine was silent. I really was puzzled, as every evening previously the noise had been consistent with moving machinery, but this time all was silence and there was no light over the door to illuminate the "NO ADMITTANCE" sign.

Suddenly Sparks appeared, running. He opened the door with his key and in his hurry left it open. Need I tell you what I did? Yes, I went in through the open door. The whole floor area was covered with all sorts of machinery and bits and pieces. Best of all, there were two gigantic wheels, bigger by far than a railway engine's wheels and not moving or making any noise but polished as bright as my mother's candlesticks.

I gazed in absolute amazement to see Sparks lighting a colossal blow lamp and pumping away at the handle. He opened the valve and a jet of flame shot out — surely, I thought, he is not going to burn the whole place down?

He mounted the ladder on the machine and, carrying the blow lamp, pushed it into the innards of the engine. He then dismounted and saw me, but smiled as he could not talk for the noise of the blow lamp. He sat down on a backless chair facing the engine and read his paper.

I plucked up courage and slowly walked towards him, half-expecting to be told to Get Out! Some little time later he got up, put down his paper, picked up a polishing cloth and advanced towards the engine. He turned two small hand levers and, wonder of wonders, the great big wheel began to revolve, very slowly the engine gave two great coughs which frightened me to death, but then no more; the wheels stopped turning.

Sparks uttered some Gaelic words which left me in little doubt that they were not complimentary. Like a shot he was up the ladder again attending to the pumping up of the blow lamp and appeared to be checking things over. Down he came and I noticed he now had a short iron round rod in his hand; this he fitted into a hole in the big wheel and strained to turn the wheel round. This he succeeded in doing and he seemed satisfied when he had turned it around. He turned to me and I thought he said: "Must fill up the air bottle". He went through a doorway and I could hear the sound of an engine starting up; not a big engine, more like a lorry engine.

Shortly afterwards Sparks returned to the main building where I was still standing in awe of the huge wheel. He picked up his paper and, having seated himself in the backless chair, resumed his study of the paper, no doubt looking at the racing section and assessing his chances if he put a bet or two on the favourite in the big race at Newmarket.

The sound of the little engine changed abruptly after some little time and Sparks shot out of his chair and through the open doorway into the room where it was housed.

Minutes later the engine stopped and Sparks reappeared and dashed up the ladder to the big engine where the blow lamp was still alight and roaring away. He repeated the manipulation with the two small levers and, wonder of wonders, the big wheel revolved and gained speed until the whole building shook with the noise.

This was enough for me — I was off home, running almost as fast as if the big wheel was chasing me, and no doubt panting in direct proportion to the noise of the big engine. This, I thought, was the end of Mallaig, and I was very pleased to see our house still standing,

56

and as I plodded my way up the stairs I was amazed to see the light was on in the lobby.

I told no-one at home of my experience as I thought this could not be the end of the matter and I was cunning enough not to involve myself when I felt that in the morning I would be told that the electric shed and half the Wee Pier were demolished.

CHAPTER
NINE

Children's Entertainments

During the summer holidays it was not difficult to amuse ourselves, and from the age of seven or eight my playground was the seashore.

Boat-building

Here, with my two chums and classmates, I was in my element. The stave of a herring barrel deliberately broken off for our needs provided the hull of a boat; the camber of the stave was ideal for the purpose as the bow and stern were already shaped for this.

Making and fitting the keel was the next problem. One of the iron hoops which encompassed the original could be pushed into a fissure in the rocks and levered backwards and forwards until the metal was sufficiently fatigued to break.

We were now left with a piece of flat iron instead of a hoop. A narrow gap in the rocks was used to repeat this process until a piece of metal about six or nine inches long was broken off.

This formed the keel and was hammered edgewise into the stave in order to provide the required stability. A stone was the hammer and one of us held the keel in position until it was firmly secured by the combined efforts of stone and colleague.

All we needed now was a mast and a sail. The mast was part of the side of a herring box which we kicked off. One of us stood in the box while the other kicked the piece off. It was then shaved to the required diameter on the very sharp edge of the movable points on the Railway.

This took some little time but when finished it was well worth the effort. The mast had to be fitted into the stave, which meant drilling a hole and pushing the mast into position.

We had no device for making the hole, but we got a piece of railway fence wire and made it red hot by pushing it into the fire at the engine shed. This fire was available at all times as it was the fire which was drawn out of the engine fire box when the engine returned to the shed after taking a train back to Mallaig. The embers were dumped at the side of the rails before the engine was put on the turntable, turned round and driven into the engine shed. (There was enough steam in the boiler for this short journey.) It took several heatings up before a hole was bored but we persevered as this was the only way we knew of making a hole.

The sail was usually made from the cover of a school jotter, and when all was assembled the ship was ready to put to sea.

We each had a boat and when all three were built we would race them across the entrance to a small bay. The bay was perfectly horseshoe shaped and we were obliged to rush round to the other side, either to await our boat or to recover it if the wind was very strong and it had arrived before us. Sometimes the wind changed direction and one or more of the boats sailed off out to sea and were lost for ever.

The game continued until all the boats were lost; this could be days or even weeks, but a second boat was never built the same year.

Hut-building

Another extra-mural sporting activity that comes readily to mind was the building of huts. Most of the schoolboys joined up in groups of two or three and, as a team, wandered along the shore looking for the necessary materials.

When the first group started their collecting, this was the signal for hut-building to start, and any useful materials left over from the previous year's huts were eagerly collected on a first-in basis. The materials were (in order of importance): iron bed ends; corrugated iron sheets; stove piping; iron pails; planks of wood; and, finally, hessian coal sacks. As the material was collected, the building took shape.

The huts were always built in the same area, where the contour of the rocks was most suitable, and the best sites were all but fought over.

The prime requirement was a smoothfaced back wall, and when the bed ends were spaced out and set at right angles to the back wall this gave us three walls almost immediately.

The planks of wood were placed across and rested on the bed ends, eventually to be covered with the corrugated iron sheets.

The remainder of our building materials were put inside; anything under cover must not be taken by another set of builders. This was some sort of law which was strictly observed.

The coal sacks were now given attention: naturally they were filthy and had to be washed. They were dragged down to well below high tide level and were slit open to make large sheets. These were put on the shore and anchored with big stones to await the cleansing tide.

After a day or two they were taken out, usually soaking wet, and were hung up on the railway fence to dry. When they were dry enough they were taken back to our hut, draped over the bed ends and finally secured by binding fence wire through the sack and round the bed end.

When this was done we had three secure walls which provided shelter and privacy. The fourth wall was made of sacking only, and this was fixed, tent-like, at the top and the extreme ends, leaving the middle open for us to go in and out. Corrugated sheets were put on top to provide a roof.

Our hut was now complete, except for the fireplace. The galvanised pail was now examined to ensure that it had enough air holes in it (it usually had more than enough or it wouldn't have ended up on the shore). It was taken in and straddled two flat stones sited against the back wall.

The stove piping was now put on top, held by two spaced stones. The handle of the pail was held up and lashed to the pipe with fence wire and any holes left open around the pipe were filled up with small stones and eventually rendered smoketight with a clod.

About half of the top of the pail was left open to let us add fuel as required. We used a piece of roofing slate as a cover. To light the fire we would go to the engine shed and take back a shovel full of red-hot embers, pour these into our fireplace and immediately return the shovel to the engine shed.

Coal was added to the fire and we all went outside to watch the smoke coming out of the chimney (or was it to get away from the smoke now billowing out of the hut, due, no doubt, to shoddy workmanship?). Any remaining planks of wood were made into bench-like seats, supported on large stones and positioned on either side of the fire.

What was the purpose of the huts? I have since wondered if the hut-building had its origins in some folk-memory of the Clearances — a throwback to the time when it was essential to provide any kind of temporary shelter for families suddenly rendered homeless.

Anyway, for us one of the purposes was to boil up our whelks (pronounced "wilks"). All that we needed was a tin can with an attached lid, some whelks, and the already-salted sea water. The tin was put on our fire and the water allowed to boil for a short time, the tin was lifted out by its lid and the water poured away. A pin, brought from home, was introduced, and the feast began.

I don't remember anyone being sick, but I do know that the biggest whelks were found very near the sewage outfall pipe and we always had big whelks!

We also did our smoking there and, despite our coughing, we eventually managed to inhale the tobacco and coal smoke.

We occasionally played cards, and if it was too dark we would take the rear red lamp from the back of the train which had just come in. As the lamp had a red glass prism we had to open the door and turn up the wick, but it served its purpose very well. We were always careful to return the lamp on our way home.

Cycling

There were very few cyclists in Mallaig, and certainly none in our age group. Nevertheless we made up our minds that we should try to make up a bicycle from discarded parts found on the shore.

The shore, incidentally, was the universal provider; all rubbish was dumped there and stayed there until the spring tide washed the shore clean again, leaving it ready for the next year's dumping.

We first of all found a frame, no wheels, no pedals. This was carried home and put in our shed. We eventually found wheels, but of different sizes; that,

63

however, was of little account. Tyres were improvised by wrapping rope around the rim, and the accompanying bump as the wheel revolved over the joint didn't matter. A piece of wood pushed through the pedal spindle made the foot rest.

Our bicycle was now ready for the road, and great fun was had riding down Davy's Brae with one foot on the "pedal", scooter fashion. The other foot acted as the brake and prevented us from running on to the rocky shore below. Of course the bike had to be pushed up the brae for the next attempt.

My brother Duncan didn't think much of this, and he decided to make up his bicycle with a large spring fitted into the triangle below the saddle. The spring was to be wound up, rather than using the brake as he went down the hill, and was to be allowed to help in going back up by having the tension released. He worked very hard at this and I remember helping him to join up bits of broken gramophone springs; the end of the spring was made red hot and, using a nail, an effort was made to make a hole.

I don't think that we ever succeeded.

Blade manufacture

Recognising the usefulness of putting articles on the rails gave my little group the idea of collecting large wood screws and nails and laying them on the track for the train to run over.

The wood screws turned into double-edged saws and the nails into knife blades, requiring only a wooden handle fitted into position and secured with a length of cord filched from fishermen repairing their nets.

We soon learned, however, that if we allowed the engine to flatten out the nails the result was as thin as a Gillette razor blade, and so a better method had to be adopted. We would wait at the line side for the shunting engine to stop, quickly dash out and put our nail in front of the wheel of the last truck — sometimes if the rail was wet the nail would be pushed off but we overcame this by using plasticine "borrowed" from school.

We were all able to produce a very presentable blade which, when rubbed on a wet stone, had a good sharp edge.

CHAPTER
TEN

Indoor Activities

How well do I remember our gramophone! This was the property of my eldest brother, Alistair (of whom more anon). As with most modern gadgets, it was bought through "*The Catalogue*", and in our house there was but one catalogue:

J.D. Williams
the Dale Street Warehouse
Manchester, England

I think Alistair agreed to buy this very modern piece of equipment and persuaded my mother to add it to her list, and he would pay for it.

Perhaps I should mention that catalogue buying was all the go in Mallaig; the customer was required to pay to the agent a certain sum each week or perhaps each month. This meant no postal order and no postage stamp to buy, just the job for Highland folk: *something for nothing*.

Anyway, the gramophone had a label on it showing a dog listening to a horn loudspeaker so it must have been *H.M.V.* (His Master's Voice).

Ours was much superior to that as it did not have a horn. The whole thing was enclosed in a wooden surround with a grilled front backed by some kind of gold-coloured material from which the sound came.

It had a turntable covered by green baize like a modern snooker table and on this the record was carefully placed. The records revolved at 78 r.p.m. and sited on top of the wooden cabinet there was a small lever marked "FAST-SLOW".

The records were very easily broken or scratched and when carefully removed from the turntable they had to be replaced in their envelopes immediately.

Our gramophone had a handle to wind it up (all mechanical things had to have a handle — like the clock on the wall), and before the sound box was carefully positioned on the record (now revolving) the machine had to be wound up — thirty turns of the handle, no more, no less.

The needles were a mystery to me; they were in a little tin box and had to be changed frequently; we had two boxes — loud and soft, and I never knew when and how they were changed, but I remember my father looking for any old ones to put a sole on my boot.

We had quite a few records and were up to date with all the new songs. I think this was due to my sisters' influence but I don't know where they got the records, unless my eldest sister brought them from Fort William when she was working there. No gramophone records were available in our village.

The Crystal Set

After a period of years, it seems to me, the gramophone fell out of favour and was superseded by the crystal set. Now, this was something I was not allowed to touch. It required the skill of a micro-surgeon.

The crystal set was basically a device consisting of a crystal, a cat's whisker and a coil of copper wire wrapped around a cardboard tube not unlike the disposable part of a modern toilet roll.

Controlled by a brown bakelite knob was a metal finger which traversed the face of the coil in sympathy with the rotation of the knob.

As if this arrangement was not complicated enough, the box housing all the foregoing had on the back two sockets clearly marked *A* and *E*. What they represented I had no idea, and although I searched for the rest of the vowel group *I O U* (I knew my vowels at this stage), I never found them.

Later I found that wires were pushed into these sockets, but what these wires did or where they went I did not know. When I was able to look at the back (when no-one was about) the sockets were empty and the wires outside the window now.

Later my father told me, after I kept pestering him, that if lightning came and struck these wires the whole house would be knocked down.

Two further sockets were at the front of the box; this arrangement was for the earphones. When I was permitted to listen in, the earphones were clamped on the side of my head more like an instrument of torture than a device designed to give pleasure.

Whilst I must acknowledge that the crystal set was the forerunner of sound broadcasting, it was never really a great success, at least not in our house.

Should anyone be foolish or thoughtless enough to walk into the room when the set was in use, this movement was enough to upset the precise contact point between the crystal and the cat's whisker, making resetting necessary.

Fiddling the tuning knob was a delicate operation. The situation could be recovered if my brothers were listening in, but if not, the earphones were removed and placed on the table to await their attention. The earphones were never very popular as they were very uncomfortable.

Latterly the set was first tuned in using the earphones and when the station was found they were put into an empty biscuit tin and the sound was amplified so that if everyone in the room was very quiet we could all listen in providing no-one moved or spoke. I clearly remember hearing "This is L.O.I.", which I supposed meant London.

The Wireless Set

Some time later our wireless arrived. Where it came from I do not know, but I remember it being unpacked.

It really looked like a wooden box with a clock-like dial and three brown bakelite knobs on the front of it with a fretwork circle above. This, of course, was the loudspeaker.

My brothers and my mother pored over the instruction booklet, all eager to have a shot at it, but it was obvious that they were somewhat out of their depth, and the book was read and re-read with many arguments as to what was what and which was where. Neither my father nor my sisters took any part in this, and I, of course, was ignored.

Wire-less was it called? The whole of the living-room floor was like a Railway wire fence.

First we had to have a new aerial. This had to be insulated and installed outside, supported by two egg insulators, one attached to the Railway telegraph pole outside the window, the other screwed to the top window sash, with a lead into the wireless set socket marked A.

Having the end of the aerial attached to the window sash gave the maximum height to the wire, but if the window was opened the wire sagged and any attempt to shut it again usually ended with the wire caught in the window and the plug pulled out of its socket.

The next wire was the earth; this was a bare wire and it was eventually concealed under the living-room wax cloth en route to the scullery. It was necessary to wrap it round the water pipe and tighten it up with pliers.

I remember my father was on his knees supervising this operation as he was afraid that the wire would either cut through the lead pipe, or at best, if too tight, might cut off the water altogether, but my brother, who had the pliers, insisted that it had to be very tight or it was no use at all.

The task was eventually completed and careful examination showed no water around the joint, and when the faucet was turned on, how pleased everyone was when water came out. Success at last, but I was disappointed when no sound came from the wireless.

At this stage my services were dispensed with and I was sent off to bed. I fell asleep listening to the occasional raised voices, and I heard the word "wireless" many times.

Next morning the wireless table was littered with batteries. The wireless had two: one a great big black slab with lots of sockets on top, and, written on the cardboard in which it was housed, was:

HIGH TENSION — 120 VOLTS

The other battery was much smaller and had only two sockets growing out of a black tar top. Written on its side was:

GRID BIAS — 9 VOLTS

All very foreign to me. But wait, there was also a tall square glass jar filled with water (or so I thought). On top of this there were two knobs, one red and another black, and it had a metal carrying handle.

Later I often had the task of taking it down to the Electric Shed to have it revitalised. Not that I understood why I had to undertake the journey, as when I was sent to collect it again it appeared to be exactly the same.

My mother would say: "Go and get the accumulator", and orders were orders and so off I had to go at the double. This order was usually given at teatime and as I got older I realised it had to do with our light going on. This, of course, told my mother that the Electric Engine had started up and that Sparks would be in attendance.

Sparks' Shed

I would ask Sparks if our accumulator was ready and in answer to my polite question he would invariably reply: "Come away ben to the wee room and we'll see if it's on the bile".

Together we would go through the engine shed, past the noisy, snorting, smoking engine which, to me, was ready to explode, and into the wee room at the back.

As soon as we were in he shut the door and that made the noise bearable. As the door shut a semi-circular area immediately behind it was swept clean, but the edge of the semi-circle was built up of empty cigarette packets. There were *Capstan, Woodbine, Gold Flake*, to name the more common ones; enough to have kept a tobacco factory busy for one day. Intermingled with these were matchboxes: *Bluebell* matches, *Puck* matches and *Union* matches. The floor reminded me of the flotsam which we children searched through on the shore after a stormy day.

72

The floor behind the high tide mark was littered with bits of wire, glass batteries on their sides, battery-carrying handles and wooden boxes for putting batteries into, kipper wrapping papers (greaseproof), hammers, nails and a miscellany of rusty tools.

Against one wall stood a sagging armchair, and on the upturned herring box (now converted into a table) stood a tin lid ashtray full to overflowing and spilling out onto the floor below.

This obviously was the sitting-room area, complete with armchair in which Sparks would recline while studying the racing form in the *Daily Record*, so that he could have a wee bet with the bookie's runner next day.

On the end wall and underneath the window there stood the dining-room table. This was made of the ubiquitous herring box, but raised up above the litter on four barrel staves, one nailed to each corner.

On top of this newspaper-covered table there stood all the kitchen equipment: a primus stove, an aluminium teapot (which I am sure doubled as a kettle, as the handle was burned through), two or three dirty enamelled mugs, a tin of condensed milk complete with teaspoon, and an open packet of Melrose Sunray tea.

The window and the windowsill were filthy and covered with spent tea leaves. This was the exit point, where the teapot was emptied; the glass in the window was so badly tea-stained that very little light was able to pass through.

A small area had been rubbed clean so that Sparks could look through and see what was going on at the pier below; perhaps I am doing him an injustice — it may well have been for him to see if it was dark enough outside for him to start up his engine.

On the right-hand side wall I was able to see several clocks (instrument dials), below which, on the floor, laid out in full regimental order against the wall, all jumbled up with bits of wire, there was an assortment of glass batteries, some big and some small.

In reply to Sparks' question: "Which wan's yours?" I pointed to the brand-new battery, the only one with a label on it. Bending down, he deftly removed it from the orderly line by yanking the wires off and, holding it up to the overhead light, pronounced: "Aye, it's fair biling".

Next we had the acid test, so to speak. He coupled up the two terminals on top of the battery with a thin piece of copper wire, and after this had glowed red hot and immediately ruptured, he declared the accumulator "well done".

"Jist you feel how hot it is and mind ye dinna spill it as ye gang home."

On my way out, carefully carrying the accumulator, I noticed a beautiful blue light on the wall above. It was bright enough to be frightening and I wondered at the time how this wonderful clear light could associate with the midden surrounding it.

Years later I learned that it was a mercury arc rectifier used to convert AC current to the DC current necessary for charging wet batteries. Lower down on the wall there was a long glass tube three or four feet long and about four inches in diameter. It was lit up and coloured pink, giving off enough heat to raise the temperature in the wee room to equal that of the boiler room in a coal-burning transatlantic liner. This glass tube, I was to learn later, was the forerunner of the modern electric fire.

The accumulator refitted

My homecoming was obviously awaited, because for once I was treated with a degree of kindness.

"Oh, good, you got it then."

The accumulator was quickly taken from me and fitted into the innards of "the set", as it was now affectionately called.

Alistair, as the owner, was privileged and was coaxed to put it on. This he did and we all surrounded him, looking at it in wondering expectancy. He twiddled all the knobs in turn and we were able to hear music. Naturally he had to turn the volume up full just to see how loud it would go, and on restoring the volume to a reasonable level, he pronounced it "very good".

He told my mother it was better than Mrs So-and-So's, but so it should be as ours was a *three valve* set. None of us knew what this meant, not even my mother, but I know we had no tea that night — we were all too busy listening in.

The wireless was a great success; we heard all the latest bands and comedy programmes, and, of course, the weather forecast and the news.

The latter was a prime favourite of my father, and when Alistair tried to explain the workings of the set to him with the aid of a handbook, how to switch it on and how to tune in, I recall my father looking at the book and saying that he would understand all about it fine if only it had been written *in the Gaelic,* and he thought it would be safer if he left it alone.

CHAPTER
ELEVEN

The Dentist and the Barber

Of all the duties and obligations imposed on me as a child, my greatest dread was having my hair cut. This was worse than being attended to by the school dentist, who, accompanied by his female nurse, paid us an annual visit.

The Dentist

The dentist and his girl assistant were equipped with charts showing teeth. First one boy volunteer came out and agreed to have his teeth examined. Each of his decayed teeth was scored out on the chart in red chalk or crayon. There were pretty few unadorned teeth left when he was allowed to leave.

Then we were all, in turn, called out of class by the nurse and she escorted us into the Holy of Holies, the staffroom.

The dentist was dressed in his white coat and he beckoned us to sit down on a chair. The nurse closed the door, and turning round, stood in front of it and watched proceedings. Although I didn't realise this at the time, on reflection I'm sure she was on guard duty and would have restrained any pupil who foolishly thought that he had had enough and tried to make a getaway.

We each had our teeth poked at and prodded, and he only seemed satisfied when our mouth, tongue or gums were bleeding very nicely. We were given a tablet and the nurse led us up to the cloakroom to ensure that we took it. There was no glass available so we were obliged to put the tablet in our bleeding mouth and suck the cold water tap, and then swallow the lot. As this was our usual way of having a drink, I for one thought nothing of it.

At the end of the day we were given a green card to take home with us, but as it only made recommendations, it was either not delivered or else ignored. Had we been warned of the dentist's impending visit, I am sure few of us would have attended school on that day.

At the end of the visit, we were all given a toothbrush, a round tin of Gibbs Dentifrice and a booklet entitled *Fight Decay Protect Your Ivory Castles*. I never used my gift, but my mother found the brush and the moistened contents of the tin very good for getting into the cracks and corners of the brass candlesticks which adorned the mantelpiece.

Only once did I have toothache very badly, and my mother, having tried all the usual cures (chewing tobacco, taking an Askit powder, going to bed with a sock full of hot salt to put on the pillow), marched me off to the doctor's to have the tooth removed. As this was a baby tooth, extraction was relatively easy and sitting in the chair was of short duration and quite a novelty. I remember boasting about it at school.

Hair-cutting

Hair-cutting, on the other hand, was accomplished by my father and I think he disliked this duty as much as I did; I am sure he was put up to it by my mother. He was of crofting stock and I suppose my mother considered he would have had some experience in sheep-shearing, a skill not unlike haircutting.

In any case, after I had had my tea, my mother would announce, "You are going to have your hair cut". There was no way out and an eagle eye was kept on me so that even a visit to the toilet was carefully monitored to ensure that I didn't abscond.

Now came the preparations. The living-room tea-table was cleared and the blanket-like cover folded up and put away, then the table was pushed against the wall, the clootie rugs were shuffled away into a corner and all the chairs, with one exception, were piled together.

Next the *Oban Times* was produced, but not to be read, of course. A hole was torn out of the middle of the paper in a somewhat circular shape and this was fitted over my head. Usually the hole was too small but the fact that my ears were all but torn off was of little consequence, as a snug fit was the prime requirement.

The remaining sheets of the *Oban Times* were put on the floor so that the hair would be collected and there would be no need to find the sweeping brush to sweep the waxcloth. The chair was carefully placed in the middle of this island of newsprint and I was seated.

My father took up his station in front of me, equipped with comb and rusty scissors. As he advanced towards me I had to press my head into his stomach so that he could cut the hair at the back of my head. This position was agonising, especially as his watch chain, which stretched across his waistcoat from pocket to pocket, fitted exactly across the front of my forehead, and the more I edged backwards the more he edged forwards to ensure that my head was immovable. Even the next day the imprint of the chain was embossed on my brow.

The shearing now began in deadly earnest and I was continually told to keep still and stop fidgeting and, while any head movement was nigh on impossible as my head was held in a vicelike grip, the fact that for each hair cut at least two were plucked made my fidgeting inevitable.

I suppose the scissors were blunt, as they were generally used to cut up the pieces of cloth or knitted wool necessary to make yet another clootie rug.

I was obliged to hold this immobile posture for at least half an hour, and for each snip and pluck my father had two puffs to remove the shorn hair around the *Oban Times* collar. Naturally, the hair was blown down my back, creating a dreadful itch, but the purpose was achieved and a new area of head was exposed, ready for the next hack with the scissors, and the swift attack with the saw-like comb.

When the back was at last finished to my father's satisfaction, he called to my mother and together they would lift the chair, while I was still sitting on it, and turn me through ninety degrees. This was in order to do the side, and the movement was essential to catch the light from the window. Fifteen minutes later it was the turn of the other side and once more my mother's help was necessary to turn me round yet another quarter-circle.

After a further session of plucking, hacking and ear-nipping and a good blowing and patting at any hair that was left, I was told "nearly finished, only the dosan (forelock) to do now".

Again I was turned around to face the window, and as the *Oban Times* carpet originally under the chair was a crumpled mess, one or sometimes both of my parents would trip, and as they regained their balance the comb or even the scissors would inflict a passing blow to my already sorely bruised head.

This was no great worry, although I was pretty well scalped in places and the blood was trickling from the nips I had endured on the sides of my head. I bravely felt the back of my head but the blood had congealed and all I could feel there were the dried clots.

The ultimate task was now to be performed and again my mother's aid was enlisted; she would grab my dosan and lift it up like a corn stook while my father fitted the comb in at the agreed height. Two or three snips with the scissors and the task was finished. My mother had the hair in her fist and I had tears in my eyes.

There was yet one more associated hazard to be endured — the application of the ointment that was vigorously rubbed into my scalp to arrest the flow of blood and promote healing, and to encourage the growth of the new crop of hair.

This concoction was an emulsion made up of paraffin and tar and had a pungent smell. Years later I learned that this preparation was used by crofters to deter the blowfly after a sheep-shearing event!

The *Oban Times* ruff was now removed and was still in pristine condition: the hairs it was designed to collect had been blown off and were now under my jersey, quite eager and happy to make me itch every time I moved.

At last I was free to go. Only once did I have the courage to stand up on a chair and have a look in the looking-glass hanging on the wall. When I did this I turned round quickly to see who it was standing behind me; I didn't recognise myself.

I was afraid to go out but had to the next day, and unbeknown to my mother, I managed to absent myself from school for several days, and even after that the paraffin smell was so pronounced that I was shunned by all the other boys, as they believed I had head lice. Paraffin was the cure for this infestation, and their belief was confirmed by my shorn hair. I did manage to get some of my brother's brilliantine and used it liberally in an effort to regain my position at school, but with little effect.

I recall grumbling to Duncan about the steps and stairs in my hair, and he considered I was making a fuss, as my father, having practised on him for years, was now quite good at the haircutting, and in any case it would soon heal up.

He, by that time, had a trim at Angus's in a shed on the pier for 3d. and I followed his good example. The first 3d. I earned or got was saved for this purpose.

CHAPTER
TWELVE

The School and
School Days

My earliest recollection of school was being taken up to the Infant Classroom by my sisters and handed over to the teacher.

Before leaving home I was given a small bottle of water and a piece of clean rag to clean my slate with.

I well remember the wooden-framed slate and the slate pencil but I don't ever remember using the cleaning rag. The usual method for slate-cleaning was very much easier; the jersey sleeve was pulled over the clenched fist, and a spit on the slate and a quick rub with the sleeve was all that was required.

As this was the standard practice, I quickly adopted this method; it did have one drawback, however, because when the slate dried it developed a white coating, and in order to make any visual impression we had to press very hard, with the inevitable result: a broken slate pencil.

As I was a new pupil I had been given a very short pencil, about two inches long. Now I had two, each one inch long. It was impossible to make any mark on the slate and the teacher was very angry with me.

I spent the rest of the lesson spitting and rubbing my slate, trying to rub off the white coating. Of course I had to wait for it to dry each time and I quite enjoyed watching and repeating the process.

Not a very auspicious start!

Mallaig boasted but one school, catering for the educational requirements of all the children aged from five to fourteen. There were three infant rooms and a like number of junior rooms all housed in one building which had coat hooks at each end, with individual doors for the infants and juniors.

Detached from the main building was the Cookery Room, really an overgrown corrugated iron structure. This was also used for drawing, music and navigation lessons and was used only by the two top classes. The centrepiece was a huge black iron range with an oven on each side of the coal fire, which was lit only during a cookery lesson.

Until such time as we sat the Qualifying Exam at the age of twelve, the lessons were very much the same as in any junior school, but after this all-important exam extra subjects were introduced.

We had lessons in navigation, domestic economy (cooking and sewing), French, algebra, geometry, science and music. These extra subjects were in addition to our usual lessons: English, history, geography, sums (tables every day), and sometimes, if the teacher was not too upset and in a good mood, physical jerks.

How this was all fitted in I do not know, but I do know we had no timetable to follow.

Nicknames

Perhaps at this stage it may be appropriate to make mention of my two chums.

We were a composite unit without any designated leader, but at all times, whatever was proposed or suggested, we discussed it, and if the odds were in favour it was carried out. We were all in the same class at school and, as was common custom in the Highlands each had a nickname.

I was familiarly known as *Johnnie Von*, but after a time the "Johnnie" was dropped and I was *Von*. Why Von? the German foreign minister, who visited Scotland about this time (1933), was Herr *von* Mackensen. This was near enough for my chums, and so I was re-christened.

The next lad, whose name was Roddy MacLean, rejoiced in the name of *Jerry*. This was because on occasion he used to wear his father's memento of World War I: the German coal-scuttle tin hat.

The last in the trio was *Dicka Burt*. I think he was of English parentage — at any rate even his mother called him Dicka, although when his name was called out for the school register it was to Richard Burt that he answered.

The nickname was used in the West Highlands, usually to distinguish father from son, so we referred to Old Donald, Young Donald, or even Red Donald or White

Donald, depending on hair colour, but every Donald, the common name, had to have an identification.

The "whipper-in"

I was very pleased when Duncan left school at fourteen as I was now the last one in the family at school and I could dodge this duty without fear of anyone clyping on me.

This was wonderful to begin with, but I soon found out it wasn't much fun wandering around alone, particularly as I had to keep an eye out for the "whipper-in" who augmented his earnings by having a casual porter's job, sometimes at the pier and other times at the station.

When there were two of us not in need of education, one would look for him at the station while the other looked for him at the pier. Naturally we chose our base depending on where he was working.

Even so, he occasionally caught me, and putting his custodial hand on my shoulder, would enquire: "Whit wey are ye no' at the school?" Convincing answers were very few:

"My mother is sick so I have to get the messages."
"We all slept in."
"I was sick in the night and my mother said I had better not go to school."

I must have appeared very convincing as I was not aware of ever being reported.

Not easy

It may well be that the reader has assumed that schooldays in Mallaig were happy days, but let me state that the opposite was nearer the truth.

Our education was one of fear and a continual battle between teacher and pupil. The strap was in daily use, and corporal punishment was considered one of the basic principles of education and rigorously applied at the slightest misdemeanour or excuse. The teacher had the strap coiled up on his elevated desk, but in my class it was rarely coiled up, as it was normally in use and often I was the reason for its use. Apart from the indignity and the classroom silence, the pain was excruciating, especially if the teacher's aim was poor and the strap curled around the wrist, which quickly doubled in size and became numb. At any rate, that hand was out of service for the remainder of the day. I recall one boy with a dreadful stammer being given four of the best when he tried to recite the verse of poetry which had been our homework.

However, this is my story of school as I remember it, perhaps I have embellished it a bit: there is a temptation to do so, and as even some of the best incidents have faded away, a little embellishment must be forgiven.

CHAPTER
THIRTEEN

English Lessons

One feature of our English lessons in the top class was sentence analysis, better known as parsing. We were to divide the sentence into subject and predicate; direct and indirect objects. These headings were put up on the board and we had to copy them into our jotters.

To measure the success of this exercise, let me elaborate. Most of my class didn't know a noun from a verb, and although we had a shot at filling up the columns, the result always made it necessary for the teacher to go back to basics.

We were told that a noun was the name of a person, a place or a thing, but as a rough guide, anything that we were able to see — boat, pier, engine, station — was a NOUN.

The rule of thumb for a verb was equally simple: a verb is a doing word, and if we could put "to" in front of the word, "to run", "to play", "to go", then that word was a VERB.

In the sentence *we go to school*, go is a verb because it has *to* in front of it, and *school* is a *noun* because we can see the school.

"Now, do you all understand?" Vacant looks; no reply. "Right, who will tell me a verb?" Long pause. At last one girl put up her hand very timidly. "Well done, Harriet. Tell the class what your verb is." "Kippers, Miss."

There was not even a titter from the class; most of us thought she might be right, and the rest had not even been listening. The teacher rose from her desk, and, to cover her embarrassment or amusement, opened the window. On her return to her elevated position she asked Harriet why she thought "kippers" was a verb. Harriet was very happy to oblige with her reason and answered, "Please, Miss, my father took two kippers to his tea yesterday, and you said if you can put to in front of a word, then it is a verb".

"But, Harriet, dear child, don't you understand? You can see a kipper, so . . ." She was interrupted by a quiet voice from one of the boys at the back: "Aye, but they canna see us." The boys roared with mirth. Poor Harriet rushed from the class in tears, closely pursued by Miss.

End of lesson — out to play.

After a great deal of trial and error the Elementary Grammar was sorted out, including the following bit of revision: "Now, you remember last week we had a lesson on nouns and verbs. Now, we all know that Angus here is a noun. We know, because we can see Angus, so Angus is a noun." Angus's reply to this was: "No, no, Miss, I'm a Catholic!"

We eventually progressed to adjectives, and a whitewashed door was discussed. On being asked what was the colour of the whitewashed door, the boy in question did not know: he hadn't seen the door!

As light relief from this strenuous work, we were subsequently introduced to Word Construction. This entailed the new words *prefix* and *suffix*. In order to master this aspect of English we were given a wee, soft-covered brown book in which we could write our own name, provided we agreed to give the teacher 6d. a week to pay for it.

The only page I ever read was the first, which told me that the *pre* in *prefix* was from the Latin meaning "before", and that the *suf* in *suffix* was really *sub*, meaning "under", as in submarine.

We went through our *pres* and *pros* and even learnt about antonyms and their meanings. We learned and were obliged to write down pages and pages of prefixes and suffixes, and one lesson was given over to the learning and writing down of:

For we must learn each pro and con
And every aspect dwell upon.

Needless to say, all this stood us in good stead and contributed in no small part to our future development.

Actually, I quite enjoyed these lessons, and, while I understood most of what we were told, I know that the vast majority of the class preferred Shakespeare's *Macbeth* or the *Merchant of Venice*.

The reading of these plays alternated with the learning of English Grammar, and we took it in turns to read two pages aloud to the class during each lesson.

CHAPTER
FOURTEEN

Arithmetic

Bearing in mind that most of the top class had failed the Qualifying, it is surprising that our teachers were so dedicated and enthusiastic.

In arithmetic lessons the decimal system was now introduced and I, for one, fully understood what this was all about. Even at my early age I appreciated how sensible this system was, and my understanding has stood me in good stead.

All metric units were explained to us and related to the Imperial system.

For these lessons rulers were given out and we learned that 30 cm. was near enough 12 inches; similarly one kilogramme was 1,000 grammes and just over 2 lbs. Liquid measurements — like litres in relation to pints — were not only taught but practically demonstrated, using milk bottles and water.

Adding and subtracting was simple, provided the decimal points were vertically in line. This was one subject I really understood, and, believe it or not, I was praised by my teacher and held up as an example: "If he can do it, anybody can". Praise indeed!

Percentages, simple and compound, were much more difficult, and while I knew that if you were given a discount of 2½% you would be given sixpence back if you spent £1, this was the only percentage that I knew, and I never really understood very much about it. Compound interest I didn't understand; it was well above me and so the lesson was disregarded.

Calculating area was something I half understood, especially in one lesson when hens were mentioned. We had hens ourselves, and I really paid attention to this. "If we have a hen-run 5 ft. long and 3 ft. wide, how many square feet does that make?" One of my chums asked how many hens were there, and on being given an approximation by the teacher, he doubled the number as he knew that hens have two feet. That was his answer! Another boy asked how far did the hens have to run, anyway.

Then we had to calculate the amount of whitewash needed to paint a wall 10 ft. high and 10 ft. long. One boy was asked what colour would the wall be. He didn't know but his mother used ochre on their walls and that was pink, except in the scullery where it was yellow. Anyway, it rubbed off if you brushed against it and you got it all over your jersey.

Lessons in algebra were quite beyond me and, to most of the boys at least, this subject was sums with letters mixed in.

Geometry was somewhat better and we did understand about angles and circles, but the use of the lines on the brass protector (as we called the protractor) was always a bit of a mystery.

The compasses were a little bit difficult and we were confused as to which leg was north but too frightened to ask the teacher. We did, however, learn to make circular patterns with them, and boys who had a knife took out the screw and then spent the rest of the lesson looking for it and putting the compasses back together again with one of the legs backwards.

Equal division

In the adult world, making the choice between two parties or two people is often done by tossing a coin while one of the parties calls out "heads" or "tails". In the case of twelve-year-olds without money an alternative method had be arrived at.

This had to be simple and as infallible as the coin method. Firstly a flat stone had to be found. In any seaside area, and certainly in Mallaig, flat stones are as much a rarity as hen's teeth. Sometimes a piece of slate would be found and, if approved, one side was licked. While the newly-licked side was still clearly seen, the stone was tossed up into the air and the cry went up: "wet" or "dry", or perhaps the call "nae birl". Should this cry be heard, the toss must be repeated and this time the thrower must ensure that the stone birled or spun while in the air.

The experienced contestant would always call "dry", because if the ground was wet, both sides of the stone would be wet, and, contrary to normal practice, he didn't want to win. Sometimes the thrower-up would "accidentally" wipe the wet side of the stone against his trousers as it was being thrown up. If the stone landed in a puddle, the person who called out "wet" won. If the stone ended up against another stone on the ground in an edgewise position, this was called "canted" and the whole procedure was repeated.

Some readers might wonder why we had all this business of throwing stones up in the air and what choices we had to make, but this was necessary in order to conform to the immutable rule which clearly and simply stated: "Him that cuts canna pick".

To explain: if one of us had gone a message for a neighbour he might have been rewarded with an apple or a penny or anything that could not easily be shared, and so the problem of equal shares became acute. If I had been given a penny, my favourite purchase was a packet of sweetie cigarettes. There were five in a packet and they were red-tipped to suggest that they were alight.

Try sharing five cigarettes with two others. We would have one each but everything had to be equally shared, and the boy who won the toss had to do the sharing. The rule forbade him to choose or to pick up any of the pieces he had cut. Needless to say, it would inevitably be the smallest that was left to the person who cut up, and this was the reason that no-one wanted to win the toss and be required to make the even distribution. All this because any penny we got was never allowed to get warmed up in one grubby hand, but had to be spent immediately. The whole process could take up to an hour at best. Perhaps I should have called this "long division".

CHAPTER
FIFTEEN

Domestic Economy

Domestic Economy lessons alternated weekly with cookery lessons. The girls, and one or two of the boys, did their knitting, while the rest of the boys had to sew on buttons.

This in itself was no mean task, as getting the thread through the eye of the needle could take up to twenty minutes, especially if about a dozen boys were helping the one holding the needle, either by looking all over the floor for it or helping to push it into a neighbouring girl.

Learning to darn socks and jersey elbows was equally daunting, and the less able spent the lesson trying to push the wool through almost invisible eyes, while others occupied their time looking for the hole in knitting needles.

The frog

Sometimes the two top junior classes shared a Domestic Economy lesson, and on one auspicious occasion my elder brother's class and mine were sharing such a lesson.

At dinner time my brother found a frog, and when the bell rang he went into the Cookery Room and placed the frog in the teacher's desk.

During the lesson the top class was much more unruly than usual, so much so that the teacher threatened the trouble-makers with the strap if they didn't behave.

Naturally they didn't and, calling out the names of the miscreants to come to her desk, she lifted the lid to get out the belt whilst keeping her eagle eye on the shuffling wretches before her, put her hand into the desk and grabbed the frog instead of the strap.

You can imagine the chaos and panic that ensued. Screaming and shaking her hands, the teacher jumped down from the podium and ran through the door, followed by all the by now hysterical girls. After we had had a very good laugh, we quietly returned to our desks and resumed our darning or sewing — we knew what was to follow.

Minutes later the headmaster barged into the now silent room followed by a retinue of girls. He was quivering with anger and red in the face. An inquest was held immediately, and if he had to give the strap to every one of the boys, he would get to the bottom of this disgraceful affair. In reply to his questions all the information given to him was:

"Oh, yes, we saw Miss go out in a bit of a hurry. "A frog? Oh, no, we didn't know she kept frogs. Has she lost one? No, we didn't see a frog." (It had been thrown out of the window.) One of the older boys said he thought he had seen one in the burn yesterday.

We were told that Miss . . . was in a state of shock and would have to go and see the doctor. The headmaster questioned the girls, the normal source of information, but for once they could not "clype" on us as the incident had not been planned beforehand. With the threat that we would hear more of this, he stormed out of the room brandishing his tawse.

After school all the boys agreed it was the best lesson we had ever had, and, although we were all apprehensive for a day or two, we heard no more about it.

Ironing

Despite our simple diversions, lessons on Domestic Economy continued, and we managed to get some ironing done.

A number of irons were put on the top of the stove, and when the correct temperature was reached (it was checked periodically by spitting on the upturned sole-plate), we were allowed to rub it over a shirt or something similar.

Any dirt on the iron was rubbed off on a wet towel; needless to say, some scorching took place, and part of the fun was to knock off the buttons on the garment. This probably contributed to the smooth running of the next lesson, as the class following had to be taught how to sew the buttons back on.

Hygiene

We were given books on hygiene, both personal and domestic. We knew the reason for using soap and washing soda and we learned that Lysol and iodine were to be used for cuts and bruises, and demonstrations in bandaging were given. We were all "given a go" at folding a triangular bandage into an arm sling and tying the reef knot behind the patient's neck. Naturally, the object of this was to show how tightly we could pull the bandage and strangle the patient while we fumbled with the ends in an endeavour to make a knot.

We also had to take our neighbour's pulse, jersey sleeve pulled up, wrist exposed. This was pressed very firmly to feel the beat. I think my neighbour must have been dead as I never did find the pulse on his wrist.

We were told about oral hygiene and the necessity of cleaning our teeth after every meal. A toothbrush was displayed; I am sure it was the first one most of us had ever seen. The suggested cleaning agent was salt.

CHAPTER SIXTEEN

The Arts and Language

I clearly remember our drawing books; they had grey pages like newsprint, separated by sheets of tissue paper.

We always used very soft crayon which was very easily smudged. I was hopeless at drawing and was very envious when I looked at some of the girls' books and compared them with my attempts.

Something called "*Still Life Drawing*" was our speciality. I remember a lone daffodil in a jam jar on the teacher's desk; this was the object of the lesson. I tried very hard to get the sides of the jar symmetrical but it was beyond my capabilities so I turned my attention to the daffodil. This proved to be even more difficult, so a quick rub-over with my sleeve sorted it all out.

I soon realised that Drawing was not my strong point and I simply had to find a means of getting out of it, particularly as on occasions my book was held up and caused great laughter in the class. I did get out of it eventually.

On one occasion the teacher had said to me, "I will do the marking in your book, and not you with your filthy hands". So I now came into the room with dirty and muddy hands and was told to go into the cloakroom and wash them before taking part in the lesson.

I did go into the cloakroom but I don't remember washing my hands, and, as the register had been marked, I did not return to the classroom. Instead I went round the back of the school and spent the rest of the day down at the pier looking at the boats and the fish. I was never caught out and was able to do this several times.

Music lessons

If the drawing lessons were a disaster, the music lessons were even worse.

From my point of view the only redeeming feature was that for once I was not alone. When we were singing my voice, like that of most of the boys, was, according to the teacher, "like a gathering of corncrakes", whatever that was.

Our singing was accompanied by the teacher playing the piano, and she had great difficulty trying to play while at the same time looking over the top of the piano to see what the boys were up to.

The girls' plaits were pulled and the rendering of *"Ho-ro, my nut brown maiden"* was interspersed with squeals from the girls and laughter from the boys.

Our singing of "*I left my baby lying there*" received similar treatment, and in the end all the boys were excluded from this cultural lesson.

Instead we had to go back to our classroom where, under the eagle eye of our headmaster, we were taught Navigation.

Language

Mallaig is a small fishing village on the north west coast of Scotland, overlooking the Isle of Skye. It is served mainly by the North British Railway Company from Fort William, a town 42 miles south.

This sentence is not of my construction; it was written up on the school blackboard when we returned after the summer holidays.

Our first task when we were settled down in the top class was to write a composition. We were issued with two sheets of paper and a pencil, a cunning arrangement as, on reflection, I am certain previous pupils would have no pencil, no jotter, and so no composition.

All this equipment had to be bought by the pupils' parents. There were two subjects that we could expand on:

1. What I did in the summer holidays

or

2. Our Village

Naturally, no. 2 was the favourite; after all, more than half was already written up on the board, and those who could read the teacher's handwriting made a start at copying it out.

Your name had to be written on the top of the paper as shown on the board:

John MacDonald — Mary Gillies and the date as shown: *1st. September 1930.*

Every paper started with John MacDonald — Mary Gillies and the date as shown — most of this was then rubbed out with a wet finger, at least all of the boys' was, and re-written with only John MacDonald left on the paper.

Next the questions would start: "Please, sir, what is that word after saved?" Whole class stops, pencil chewing begins. Teacher looks at board, reads it through under his breath.

"The word *saved* is not on the board; it is *served.*"

SERVED is written up on the board in capital letters.

"Now, get on with your composition . . . Now what?"

"Please, sir, I don't know what served manly means." This is explained and *MAINLY* is printed up on the board. Girl's hand shoots up.

"Now what?"

"Please, sir, my father served in the Navy in the War."

"Yes, yes, I am sure he did. Now, get on with your composition."

Quiet for two minutes, more questions asked and answers given. At last the bell rings for playtime.

"Stop, (some hadn't even started) hand in your papers and go out to play."

End of English lesson.

In the top class English and French were taught almost as one subject.

During the French lessons I learned about personal pronouns, both singular and plural, and as we learned French verbs we also had to know about tenses.

We started off on the verb *to be* and learned *I am* right through to *they are*. We learned this verb up to the future tense and then went on to *donner* — to give.

In addition to the verbs we also had lots of French nouns to memorise and had to copy them from the textbook into our jotters. This was for homework.

This was a subject I liked and I was pretty good at it. I gave up when we came to reflexive verbs in the negative; this was too much for me; perhaps Gaelic would have been easier. Try saying "Cha n-eil mi a' dol an cadail" in French when you are a thirteen-year-old-boy in Mallaig!

History and Geography

History and geography lessons were mainly devoted to Scottish affairs and were very boring. We were required to remember the names and dates of battles: Culloden, Bannockburn, Prestonpans and so on, and of course we learned about Bonnie Prince Charlie and Flora MacDonald.

The MacDonalds featured again in the Massacre of Glencoe, and woe betide any Campbell in the class; retribution by the MacDonalds at playtime was the best part of this particular lesson.

Geography meant learning the names of all the Scottish counties, all the mountain ranges and the rivers. Writing these from the blackboard occupied most of our lessons.

As a slight diversion we did occasionally have a lesson on the colonies. This meant a tatty world map being thrown over the easel and the colonies pointed out to us. This was a simple matter as they were all coloured pink. Nevertheless we had to write the names in our jotters.

One of the rooms in the Junior section was the Science Room, and, on reflection, I think it was very well equipped. It had tables and stools instead of desks, and rows of shelves. One wall was given over to sinks and draining boards and, on the shelves above, balances were housed in glass cases. This room doubled as the classroom for the top class.

Cookery

The day before our cookery lesson we were told to arrive with all the required ingredients and, of course, a clean plate.

As far as I can remember, we started by making pancakes, and after blowing away the dirt on top of the stove we spooned on a dollop of the mixture. From this we progressed to scones, then little round cakes, and finally we all made a Christmas cake.

I enjoyed these lessons and it was my duty to ensure that the ingredients which each boy had were correctly weighed out.

When this was done satisfactorily they were put into a mixing bowl, according to the instructions on the blackboard. During the time that our cakes were in the oven we had to wash up our utensils and replace them in the press.

At going home time we had the results of our efforts put onto our plates to take home with us.

My mother was always well pleased and congratulated me on my success. Little did she know that on our way home we boys always took the best from the girls' plates and substituted our worst.

CHAPTER
SEVENTEEN

Science

Science was a subject in which I was interested and I was keen to learn more about it, and so, when I was obliged to return to school after the summer holidays and my twelfth birthday, I went back with less resentment than usual because of the science lessons, in which even my brother Duncan showed a kindly interest.

Science was taught only to the top two classes and we were introduced to it by the headmaster on the very first day after our return to school.

The class was assembled and we were made to sit on stools with the science tables in front of us.

When the Head arrived, silence fell immediately. He came through the door complete with his tawse which he flicked in front of him, coming to a standstill in front of us, pulling the strap through his semi-clenched left hand. He put the tawse on the table in front of us and addressed us in a very serious voice:

"Science is a subject that demands the greatest attention, and during my lessons I will not be interrupted. I will answer no questions because none will be asked.

"The last fifteen minutes of the lesson will be used up by clearing up any doubts you may have in your mind and by putting away any apparatus which we may have used. However, you should be able to understand all you are required to know, and to achieve this I must have your full attention.

"Should I find anyone misbehaving or daydreaming, my friend here (he stroked his belt at this stage, as affectionately as if it were a kitten) with my help will remedy any errors in behaviour."

We were required to sort ourselves into groups of four: two boys and two girls at each table.

When we had done this, however, the headmaster immediately exchanged one of the boys in each group with one from another group.

This, we were told, was to be our group for all science lessons. At a later date he would appoint a leader in each group, this leader to be responsible for the careful and proper use of all apparatus.

I was more than disappointed and even afraid of this approach, particularly so as Duncan had told me that this was the best lesson in the whole school, and that everyone liked it. I certainly didn't think much of it so far.

The first lesson consisted of learning the names of the various objects which were shown to us, and, to ensure that we had spelled them correctly, the blackboard was turned round on the easel and all the words were now on display: *beaker, pipette, thermometer, Bunsen burner* and many other "foreign" words. We had been given a science jotter each and the words had to be copied out. "But do not use the graph side; that will come later."

At the end of the lesson, which was always the last in the school day, we had a little "conflab" and wondered what this "Graff side" was, eventually consoling ourselves by hoping it would arrive in time for the next lesson and that we would be allowed to use it.

At the end of this first lesson there was very little equipment to put away and so the head asked: "Now, any questions about today's lesson?"

One of the girls, Evelyn MacLean, asked about heat and the sun, and the headmaster really opened up. We had the sun and the moon, the stars, the rotation of the earth, etc., etc., so much so that despite the shuffling of feet we were kept in until he had finished answering.

This was about half past four. Needless to say, Evelyn had a rough passage home, and no more questions were ever asked.

As the science lessons continued I was very surprised to notice the change in classroom attitude. We were allowed to watch things being done, and even, on occasion, to do things ourselves.

Heat

Our first topic was heat, and we were told that when metal was heated it grew in size and that this was called "expansion". "Now, write that word in your book."

We were informed that most materials expanded when heated, but some more than others. "You will have noticed," the headmaster told us, "that the rails on the railway do not meet each other, but leave a gap. No, this is not because the engineer did not have a ruler and made the rails a wee bit too short. If he had not left the gap, when the rails got very hot in the summer time they would expand and become longer and, instead of the rails buckling up, the gap would now close and everything would be all right. However, not only would the rail expand and become longer along its length, it would also grow larger in height, and to overcome this further problem, wooden "keys" were put in to hold the rail in position, and wood being softer than the iron rail, it would allow the rail to expand without causing any trouble."

I was very taken with this information as I thought I knew all about the rails and railway: more than most, as my father was Permanent Way Inspector.

When I told him about the science lesson we had had at school his reply was: "Aye, aye, that's right. Did he work on the railway?"

The following science lesson was a continuation of the previous topic. This time we were told we would have a Practical Demonstration proving the statements of the previous lesson to be true.

The First Experiment

On the headmaster's table he had a primus stove, and a metal handle ending in an open circle through which he dropped an iron ball.

He told us this was a Spanish cannon ball (but with hindsight I am sure this story was told for effect). He

110

called one boy forward and told him to drop the ball through the metal aperture. This the boy did successfully several times.

The primus stove was then lighted with meths and when it was pumped up and going very nicely the cannon ball was placed on top over the gauze on the tripod. ("Write these words in your jotters.")

The pupil still out in front was handed a pair of tongs and told to pick up the ball and put it through the metal ring. This he managed to do and the ball was replaced over the stove to be reheated.

When we had finished writing the new names in our jotters, the boy was asked to put the ball through the ring; this time he met with no success, try as he might.

We were told that this proved that by heating the ball we had caused it to expand ("I hope you have all written this in your books").

The teacher went one step further, however, and asked the boy to drop the hot ball into a pail of cold water which had obviously been prepared beforehand. On picking the now cold ball out of the pail, he was told to drop it through the iron ring. This time he was able to do so and we all enjoyed our first practical lesson.

Temperature

We were told that in the following science lesson we would look at thermometers in some detail. I looked forward to this, but my anticipated pleasure was soon replaced by apprehension when we were told that we would make a drawing showing the various types and different scales of each.

Drawing, as you may recall, was my *bête noire* and the only scales I knew were herring scales. I certainly was downcast and I could see that my interest in science would soon be at an end.

The following week we were told to get our science books and copy from the board using "this side of the book". A science book was held up and the graph side was pointed out.

THERMOMETERS

Centigrade:
Boiling point of water:100 degrees
Freezing point of water: 0 degrees

Fahrenheit:
Boiling point of water: 212 degrees
Freezing point of water: 32 degrees

Making the drawing was fairly easy as I could use the vertical lines on my graph paper, and the end of my pencil, carefully drawn round, represented the bulb housing the mercury.

The freezing point was marked 32° at the bottom and boiling point marked 212° at the top.

A small bottle of mercury was handed round the class and I was very surprised to notice how heavy it was. We were told that this was a metal and it was one of the very few liquid metals; it noticed changes in temperature very quickly and showed this by expanding up the very fine tube which we had shown in green in our drawing.

We were then shown a room thermometer with the scales marked on the wooden mounting; one side showed degrees C, the other was marked degrees F.

We were next shown a thermometer which was housed in a velvet-lined wooden box. This was a Réaumur thermometer with a scale 0 degrees to 80 degrees. This thermometer was no longer in common use.

Finally, mention was made of the clinical thermometer as used by doctors when we were ill: a healthy person's temperature should be 98.4 but could be much higher than this should he or she be ill.

In order to check whether we had understood the difference between Fahrenheit and Centigrade, the headmaster said: "Last night I heated up some water until it was nearly boiling; I used my thermometer and saw the mercury had risen up until it showed 85 degrees. Now, Dougal, I want you to tell me what scale this was". Dougal was one of the brighter boys but his reply was disappointing: "Don't know, sir."

"Why not, Dougal?"

"You never showed us the fish, sir! If you had brought the fish I would know straight away, sir."

Nods of assent from the rest of the boys. Amazingly, at the time we all thought Dougal was right; after all, his father was a fisherman and had shares in a boat.

During one lesson a thermometer was accidentally broken and we had a good time playing with the little balls of mercury and trying to pick them up.

Sound

From heat we went on to sound and we had the experiment using the bell jar, the suction pump and the alarm clock; the latter had a hammer on top which struck the bell on the clock.

When most of the air was sucked out, the ringing of the bell became very much quieter and latterly, though we could see the movement of the hammer, there was no sound.

We had created a vacuum, and neither sound nor heat can travel through a vacuum. Mention was made of a thermos flask (which the headmaster called a Dewar flask) and liquids were kept hot when in this flask because of the lack of air between the two glass walls. Such a flask interior was shown to each group in turn but we were not allowed to touch it. No doubt the fate of the thermometer was uppermost in the headmaster's mind.

The experiments had to be written up in our jotters, with supporting drawings on the "Graff" side of our books. The only readily identifiable object in the bell jar experiment was the alarm clock, but some of the boys had the numbers 0–100 on the dial whereas others managed to get up to 212.

Magnets

The next science lesson we had was all about magnets; this took up two or three lessons, and as a great deal of writing and drawing was necessary, I, for one, was not too keen on this topic.

We did use iron filings on pieces of glass and held a bar magnet underneath; magnetic poles were mentioned and attraction and repulsion were explained.

At the end of the lesson the newly appointed group leader was required to collect in the magnets and the iron filings, and while the headmaster was able to replace all the magnets in their wooden boxes, there were very few iron filings to be returned. They had all fallen onto the floor.

When the group leader returned the almost empty jars to the headmaster, he looked at them all in turn. I was not the only boy who expected trouble, but he came to our table, and with a bar magnet "swept" the floor and when a good "whisker" of filings was collected, these were brushed off into the jar.

We were then each given a bar magnet and made to collect the remaining filings on hands and knees. We were even made to stay in after school to finish the job to his satisfaction.

Mixtures

As our science lessons proceeded, we were given things to do. Sugar solutions were made up by each group and a new word was introduced into our vocabulary, and, of course, written into our jotters: *dissolve*.

Sand and water mixtures were also made up, but although we stirred and stirred, the sand settled to the bottom of the glass. The glasses were labelled and put to one side and left until the next lesson.

When, the next week, we "went to science" again, the water had gone and crystals had appeared in the glass labelled "sugar solution".

We wetted our forefinger and dipped it into the crystals, and on tasting it we all agreed it was sugar. The sand mixture, however, was now dry sand. We were told that evaporation had taken place.

Weight

Our final science lessons were on weight. The balances were taken out of their glass cases and each group was given one.

They were made of two metal pans which could be suspended by turning a knob in the front. (Most of the fun was twirling the knob to make the pans jump up and down.)

We were also given a wooden box of gramme weights, some like little bits of tin and others, much heavier, made of brass.

They all had a knob on top and were lifted out of their individual compartments with the forceps which were in the box.

A tin tray on the master's desk provided materials which we could use to weigh. These ranged from bits of broken pencils to drawing pins, safety pins, nails, rings and beads; each one, when weighed and recorded in our jotters, had to be returned to the tray.

I now wonder how accurate this weighing business was, as I didn't know the difference between grammes and milligrammes; somebody said it had to do with English pound notes!

During the whole series of science lessons not one boy misbehaved nor did anyone have the strap, something which was unheard of in our class.

CHAPTER
EIGHTEEN

Navigation Lessons

It was the practice for the two top classes to be taught together, and so it was the only lesson I shared with my brother Duncan, who was two years older than me.

Navigation lessons concerned the theory of navigation rather than the practical aspects. We were taught about tides, winds, currents, navigational aids, the compass, distress flares and the Rules of Seamanship. We were not greatly inspired by the lessons but they made a change.

The Caledonian Canal closed

During one memorable lesson, when our class were learning the rudiments of the compass and making a sketch of this instrument in our jotters, noting particularly the cardinal points, Duncan's class was involved in more active pursuits.

Duncan was singled out to come to the front of the class and given the task of piloting a fishing boat from Mallaig to Inverness. He was given a wooden pointer to indicate the route on the map of Scotland which was draped over the easel. He was required to give a commentary during this exercise and started off very well:

"Leave Mallaig on a westerly course, passing the harbour lighthouse on our port beam, head into the Sound of Sleat."

He then altered his compass bearings to due north with a view to going through the narrows at Kyle of Lochalsh.

As Duncan said "Kyle" the headmaster roared out, "Stupid boy, stupid boy", snatched the pointer and shouted out, "When you enter the Sound of Sleat you must steer south round Ardnamurchan Point, through the Sound of Mull and up the Caledonian Canal".

This he emphasised with frantic pointings at the map. "Telford built that canal for that very reason."

The commotion aroused even the dullest boys in my class; this was much better than drawing a compass.

Duncan, very calmly for once (he had a very quick temper), took over the pointer, saying: "If we go south your way we will have to go to the South of England, through the Channel into the North Sea, and back up the whole of the east coast to Inverness".

"What do you mean, boy? That would take weeks! You must go through the Canal."

Duncan replied, "I cannot do that, Sir, there is a big notice at the pier saying the Canal will be closed for six weeks to carry out repairs and the Harbour-Master reminded me of this when I got clearance to sail. But, if we go your way we will need more fuel and food, and, as you say, Sir, it will take weeks and we'll no' catch many fish".

The headmaster was at a loss for words, but he did have the grace to say that, if the Canal was closed, Duncan's route was the obvious alternative. Actually, the Canal *was* closed and the notice to that effect was prominently sited outside the Harbour-Master's office.

The compass

Towards the end of one of our navigation lessons we were told by our teacher that next week's lesson was to be a detailed study of a genuine seagoing instrument, and it was his intention to bring along a seagoing compass.

Sure enough, the following week as we marched into the classroom he was seated at his desk with a square polished wooden box before him.

When we were seated and silence reigned, he explained that the compass needle always pointed to the North Pole, even on board a ship in very stormy weather; however, as the boat dipped and rolled, the compass needle could be deflected and it was very difficult to plot a course under such conditions.

To overcome this problem a special compass had to be constructed which would remain upright irrespective of weather conditions. "In this box I have such a compass," he told us, and we would be allowed out in pairs to have a look at it. He explained that the dial was mounted on gimbals and that this device allowed the face to remain in the correct and level position.

As we came out the lid was opened and, sure enough, there was a very nice clock sitting on a lovely green bed. He waggled the box about but he held it up too high for us to see what was happening, and, after a final short talk, we were dismissed.

Outside in the playground Hamish MacNeill was holding forth: "He must think we're daft — there was no hands on the thing and the face was so slack it was wobbling all over the place".

"We have a better clock than that at home, but it only has one hand and it doesn't go," said Dougie Morrison.

"Did you see him shaking the thing?" asked someone else, "he didn't even have the key to wind it up."

"He even said 'box the compass' — he meant the compass was in the box," said another.

"That's right," said somebody else, "him and his gymballs — there wasnae room in yon wee box for wee marballs. I never saw any balls in it, anyway, he was just trying to have us on."

This was the final pronouncement on the seagoing compass.

Lessons in the Scout Boathouse

I found navigation lessons much more interesting when taught in the Scout boathouse. All the boys in the top class were members of the Sea Scouts and here we learned the practical aspects; all about lighthouses and lifeboats (even Grace Darling was mentioned).

We learned how to splice ropes and tie knots, rowing in a small dinghy and manning a sailing boat.

Our tutor was the local Customs and Excise officer, a man very well versed in this subject; no doubt he was an ex-naval officer.

We had a proper uniform consisting of a navy-blue fisherman's jersey with Sea Scout emblazoned in white on the chest, a round hat with a white top and the band around it printed with *Sea Scout* in gold letters. This completed the outfit and we all looked very smart.

Our weekly visit to our boathouse was always well-attended and here our lessons were held, around our boat sitting on its cradle. This was a proper ship's lifeboat and was complete with main- and jib-sails.

Occasionally we would gather at the boathouse during weekends and school holidays to launch the boat. The cradle ran on rails just like the proper lifeboat, the mast was put up, the keel dropped, the rudder put on, the flag unfurled, the sail hoisted, and off we would go for a sail around the bay. This was the part we most enjoyed.

Signalling

Morse code and Semaphore signalling were taught, too, and one week we were to be taken out on Semaphore signalling practice, providing we learned the flag positions during the week.

When the day arrived we were all present and assembled in good time at the boathouse. We collected our flags, half of which had red stripes on a yellow background, the others black stripes on a white background, and off we hurried down the shore, complete with flags.

We were divided into two groups and spaced about 50 yards apart. One group was to send the message, the other group to read it and the activity was to change at half-time.

I knew I was handicapped from the start as I was very short-sighted and wore glasses. Usually one lens had been broken and fallen out and the other would be cracked. This was the situation while we were flag waving. I could barely even see the group I was supposed to read from, and I certainly couldn't see any flags.

However, I felt I did quite well at sending our message. When we returned to the boathouse the Scoutmaster said he could make more sense of reading washing blowing about on the clothes line on a windy day. He thought we would be better to learn to send smoke signals like Red Indians.

Smoke Signals

Smoke signals — now that was a thought — why didn't we have a go at that?

My three pals and I talked it over and decided next Saturday was the day to try it out. We arranged to meet at the station complete with matches and an old coat or something similar which we could put on the fire to control the smoke.

One of the team said he could get a coat if I would help him, and on the Friday evening we "collected" a fisherman's oilskin smock which was hanging on some fishing boxes at the pier. This we rolled up and hid in an empty coal wagon at the station before going home for our tea.

Next morning we met as arranged; the matches were produced and one was lit to ensure they weren't wet, the oilskin was examined and pronounced suitable for our purpose, and off we went up the railway for about a quarter of a mile. Here we left the railway and climbed up the hillside.

We collected a very large heap of heather and set fire to it. The fire burned very quickly and we had to collect whole armfuls of heather and soon had a very good fire blazing away with lots of smoke. We held our smock above this but, needless to say, it caught fire immediately and burned even more fiercely than the heather. Despite our efforts to stamp it out we had little success, as each time we thought it was extinguished it burst into flame again and so our stamping had to be renewed.

The story of Indian War Dancing was re-enacted, without the hooting. The myth was exploded: the Indians were not dancing; they, like us, were trying to put out their signal fire which had got out of control and was threatening to destroy the village.

Unknown to us, the fisherman's smock was impregnated with fish oil, which has a flash point similar to paraffin, and this was the reason it burned so readily.

While our attention was focused on the burning smock, the heather fire had gained the upper hand and, although we tried to put it out, this proved to be beyond our best efforts, and soon the whole hill was on fire and we had to abandon our War Dance and leave the fire to its own devices.

We ran over the hill and onto the road on the other side, and after sitting down and having a drink at the roadside burn while we regained our breath, we nonchalantly walked back to the village in time for dinner.

Later in the afternoon my father came home and announced that he was late because a spark from the 11.25 train had set the hill on fire, and he had had to call his men out. With some difficulty they had managed to beat it out. So much for our smoke signalling!

CHAPTER
NINETEEN

Sports

It was at about this stage in my education that we were told that the navigation lessons were to be replaced by sport, or more specifically, football. This was to start the next week and continue each week unless it was very wet.

Most of the boys in the class were jubilant and, as we were in the top class now, the boys in the lower class would help to make up the teams.

I said most of the boys were delighted; I, for one, was not. I was hopeless at all games, but especially at football. If I played while wearing my glasses they were sure to be knocked off and broken, or if I took them off I could barely see the ground, far less the ball. Either way I couldn't win. As it happened, my worry was unfounded; we never did play a game of football!

The football pitch

When the first day for sports arrived, the two classes of boys were assembled and we had a lecture, not about football, but all about making a football pitch!

There just was no flat piece of ground within miles of Mallaig, and any football played was played on the road, with jerseys for goal posts.

We were told, however, that "Big Annie", one of the crofters, had agreed to let us use one of her fields (I should have said "piece of land").

This field was about half a mile outside Mallaig and consisted of a quagmire which collected all the rainwater from the road above. In addition to this, the ground sloped so badly that it was almost impossible for a football to remain stationary on any part of it.

Our first task, we were told, was to level the ground off, leaving a gully on the roadside for the rainwater to drain away, and to achieve this we had to collect stones and progressively build up the low end.

Now we were to follow the teacher up to the "football pitch" and to follow in a quiet and orderly column. This was an unnecessary requirement as the headmaster was going to follow behind on our first visit.

The boys in the two top classes numbered about twenty, and as we plodded along we were able to chatter amongst ourselves as we straggled on up "Annie's Brae" on the road to Morar and to our destination, better known as "Annie's Field".

When we arrived at the field we were told to go in pairs and collect as many stones as we could; this we did with a fair degree of enthusiasm and soon a fair pile was accumulated at the bottom end, ready for the teacher to position as necessary. When we were told to stop and go back and collect our books ready to go home, I, for one, was quite sorry as I had really enjoyed our football lesson.

If I remember correctly, we made four or five journeys to Annie's Field, but the novelty soon wore off and in any case it was often raining and so we couldn't go; the stones got more difficult to collect as it meant going further to collect them. Some of us spent the whole afternoon up on the field and contributed only two stones about the size of hen's eggs. This, coupled with the grumbling about sore feet, broken laces, the need to have a rest, and any other excuse, made it an impossible enterprise and so the whole idea was abandoned.

However, our efforts were not in vain, as about this time a sports committee was formed in the village and the field was eventually levelled off and grassed over by the local volunteers, but by this time I had left school and although I did occasionally watch a football match I never took part in one.

In place of our football excursions we were allowed to play games on the school playground. The girls did their skipping, both individually and in group formation, and played peevers using pieces of slate which were kicked into chalk squares on the tarmac. The boys played rounders or tig and some even played cricket: the wickets were chalked on the school wall and naturally there was quarrelling as to whether a person was out or not.

Smoking

I took little part in these activities, and one event comes to mind which is perhaps worth telling. The shelters and toilets were at the far end of the playground and made up of girls' toilets, girls' shelter, boys' toilets and boys' shelter. The whole was one large building, measuring some fifty feet in length. The shelters were not unlike garages, but were open-fronted, and had no windows but had wooden seats on three sides. The boys' toilets had two cubicles with a window in each, and individual doors. The doors were so designed that about a foot gap was left at the top and bottom.

One games day two of my mates and myself decided to have a smoke and slipped off, one at a time, into the toilet, bolted the door, got the fags out and started our smoking session. We had nicely settled down when a master rattled the door: "Come out, you boys, I know who is smoking in there and you will be severely dealt with". We were all very frightened and our only response was to pull the flush.

He put his two hands on top of the door in order to pull himself up and look in; one of us touched his hands with our lighted cigarette. The hands disappeared and he roared in pain. We kicked the window out and, in turn, dived out at the back of the toilet block and joined some boys who were playing tig.

By this time the master had recovered sufficiently to come out of the toilet, sucking each hand in turn, and pounced on us. Naturally we denied any knowledge of the incident and, of course, we were backed up by the rest of the boys who swore we had been playing with them all afternoon. We were always on our best behaviour in his class after this, but as we were leaving in two or three weeks' time, we managed to escape retribution. He made no secret of the fact that he knew the boys who had been smoking and had burnt him, and he referred to this incident almost daily without actually mentioning names.

Alcohol

Towards the end of my school attendance it seems to me that we had visits from several organisations that were determined to add interest to our schooldays and equip us better for a fuller life. The visit I best remember was the one we had from the Salvation Army. We were lectured very thoroughly about the dangers of strong drink. This was a very acceptable event, as for the first time we had photographic slides and a magic lantern. The windows were covered over and great sport was to be had as the slides were changed in the darkened atmosphere. Towards the end of one lecture we had a sing-song, with musical accompaniment provided by a girl with a tambourine. We were encouraged to join in the refrain of one of the songs: "Lips that touch whisky will never touch mine!"

CHAPTER
TWENTY

Tests and Examinations

Towards the end of each school year we were required to sit a test. This was one paper made up of ten questions covering each of the subjects we had been taught. We were allowed one hour to complete the paper. In an effort to prevent cheating, a boy and a girl were made to sit together at a desk.

When we were seated and a degree of order had been established, sheets of paper and a pencil were placed in front of each of us, and we were asked to write our name and the date on the paper. The blackboard was covered over with the tatty world map, and after he had consulted his watch the teacher whipped it away to display the test questions. "You may start now."

The girls cuddled their left arm round their paper and the boys craned their necks in an effort to copy from their neighbours without devoting any time to reading the questions on the board.

I was usually one of the first to finish, having had a shot or a guess at one or two of the questions. I usually got the Massacre of Glencoe confused with the 1745 Rebellion, and on one occasion, when naming the three

English forts in the Highlands, I managed to write Fort William, Fort Augustus . . . I couldn't remember the third (Fort George), so wrote, hopefully, *Fort Night*. I made little attempt to answer any of the other questions, and when you're required to sit on a hard seat for the best part of an hour, straining to look at your neighbour's paper without being able to see it, time passes very slowly.

In the last test before the Qualifying Exam I managed to double my usual score and gain 10 out of 50. This was due not to a sudden burst of skill, but a little bit of cunning, as I managed to get a wee look at my neighbour's paper. As I bent down to recover my deliberately dropped pencil, I nipped her leg. When she bent down to rub her injury, she dropped her guard and I had a look at her exposed paper. I was unable to repeat this ploy, as ever after she and all the other girls sat sideways with their legs outside the desk.

At last the order came: "Pass in your papers and pencils and go out to play".

I was usually first out and a *post mortem* was carried out on the exam. I took little part in this as I couldn't remember what the questions were, far less the answers.

The Qualifying Exam

The Qualifying Exam. I just had to pass. Passing it meant a daily hurl in the train to attend High School at Fort William and back home at tea time. What more could a boy wish for?

I took preparations for this event very seriously and, having been told at Sunday School that prayer could overcome any problem, provided one prayed enough, I allowed about a week and had a prayer each night to bring about a miracle and ensure my success. To double my chances I spoke to Betty Mac . . . , the cleverest girl in the class, and told her I would sit behind her in the exam and she must whisper the answers to me . . . or else!

Having hedged my bets I came to the exam, very confidently. The desks were in rows, alternately occupied by a boy and a girl. I waited for Betty to sit down and I followed and took up my station directly behind her. As the exam progressed, I whispered each question number to her and awaited her whispered reply. She readily complied and I was elated at the success of my scheme; for the first time in any exam I managed to write on both sides of the paper, and for the first time in any exam I was not the first out of the door.

I was really put out at the result. I had bargained on being in the first five, but when the papers were returned I had been awarded three marks: one for the correct date, one for writing my name correctly, and the third for legible writing. All the rest was rubbish, and in front of each question, written in red ink, was 0/5. No daily hurl in the train for me, despite my careful planning.

As was to be expected, Betty Mac . . . was given the highest marks in the exam. No doubt she had told her parents about my threats and she was advised accordingly. She never did go to Fort William school; her family left Mallaig before the new term started.

CHAPTER
TWENTY-ONE

The Morar Boys

Returning to school after the long summer holiday was always accompanied by a sense of resentment and hostility, but the year after my ignominious failure in the Qualifying Exam my return to school was accompanied by additional emotions of anxiety and apprehension; I had boasted to my peers that that was to be my last year at Mallaig school and that it was Fort William for me. Little imagination is required to understand my reluctance to attend school on the first day, but this was one attendance that was not to be missed.

The top two classes were assembled in the science room (we had no hall) and the headmaster greeted us with his usual superior grin; new teachers were introduced to us: "This is Mr (or Miss) So-and-So who will look after you for Drawing", or Music, or some such specialised subject. On reflection it seems to me that after a year's serious but futile endeavours most of the teachers gave up the struggle and moved on to more fertile areas.

This year three boys from Morar were to attend our school, as their school taught children only up to the age of twelve. The new boys would arrive on Monday and it was hoped that we would welcome them and be kind and helpful to them. Finally we were given the usual pep talk — we were now Senior Pupils and, as such, we would be expected to set a good example to the younger children.

Towards the end of the week I somehow got to know that the Morar boys were big lads and that they each had a split new bike. Sure enough, when I arrived at school on Monday a crowd had gathered in a corner of the playground. Pushing my way forward, I was able to see the reason for the assembly: three bicycles, each brand spanking new, and each firmly held by a big lad. The Morar boys had arrived.

One of the older boys, in the class above mine, was actually touching the gleaming handlebars and calling out: "Gie's a shot on your bike!" while another boy nearby asked if he could have a go, and that he could go on his father's bike but he couldn't reach the pedals.

The Morar boys grouped together and took up an aggressive stance and, in the following silence, the biggest of the three boys said: "You can have a look, but you can't touch". For myself I was content to have a long and envious look: real pedals, two brakes, a proper saddle marked *Brooks Genuine Leather*, and fixed to the back of the saddle was a pouch with a metal turnbuckle fastener, and on the down tube a pump was fitted.

As if all this was not enough, the bikes even had a carrier above the back mudguard, complete with leather straps for holding the school books. I was greatly impressed and very envious.

Soon the teacher came out to see why we hadn't gone into the classroom when the bell had been rung. Sizing up the situation, he told the cyclists to put their bikes in the cookery room until going-home time.

Later in the week I got quite friendly with one of the boys and he gave me his bicycle handbook to look at. This occupied my time and interest for two or three lessons: I learned all about chain and brake adjustments. What I didn't understand was the bit about oiling the free wheel. Why one of the wheels was free I didn't know and the book didn't say if it was the front or the back wheel.

I got friendly with the smallest of the trio: Donald Morar. The other two were Angus Morar and Hughie Morar, or at least this was the name we knew them by, but they were not the names they answered to when the register was called.

In school it was necessary to call out both the Christian and surnames as most boys were called Donald or Angus. After some time the name Morar was contracted to Mor. Donald Mor was, as I said, the smallest one, and at the age of twelve he took size seven in boots. He told me that the bikes were given by the education authorities so that they could attend Mallaig school, but they had to be given back at the beginning of the holidays to be checked over and mended if necessary.

Reflection

The Morar boys were never really accepted by us, and as a result they formed a distinct, non-integrated and almost hostile group. There were several reasons for this non-acceptance, most notably their clothes.

All the local boys wore fisherman's type navy-blue jerseys, complete with pearl buttons and, usually, darned elbows and frayed cuffs. Some cuffs were nicely glossed, as they performed the duty normally associated with a handkerchief.

The Morar boys wore identical grey herring-bone tweed jackets. Years later I learned that their uniform was provided by the parish and that the boys were either from very poor families or were fostered out. The latter practice was widely used in the Highlands; it gave the foster parents some extra money and, of course, free labourers to work the croft.

Another reason for our lack of intimacy was that all conversation between the Morar boys was in Gaelic, which most of us didn't understand, and when they did try to speak to us (usually to ask us a question), their English was so bad that we could rarely understand and it ended up with us having a good laugh at their efforts, something not exactly conducive to a good relationship. Finally they teamed up together, almost like Siamese triplets.

I recall one day in class when one of them stood up and hesitantly said to the teacher: "I want to go out, Missus". (They called all female teachers Missus and all male teachers Mister.) He was told it would soon be playtime and he couldn't go out just yet. I vividly recall his answer: "Then can I go in that corner over by the press?" The teacher quickly relented and told him he could go out, but not to be long.

As he got out of his desk he was joined by his two mates and all three made for the door. There seemed to be some confusion at the door, and in the end the teacher had to open it for them. At playtime I asked Donald Morar what the fuss and bother at the door was all about and he told me they didn't have these knob things on the doors at Morar, they had snecks, and they were trying to lift the knobs to open the door, but that didn't work; they must have been broken and they couldn't get out.

Morar school was really a drab, corrugated iron hut situated on the roadside almost opposite the cemetery. This place of interment served Mallaig as well as Morar. Donald told me he missed the funerals with all the folk and sometimes even flowers.

I am sure their whole school attended every funeral in spirit and that they were far more interested in the dead than in the living. (I was tempted to say "quick", but there was nothing very quick about the Morar folk.) I say this because I am quite sure that the Morar boys were much more than twelve, more like fifteen, and if they were fostered out, their records must either have been lost or written in English. The skill necessary to read these was beyond the capabilities of their "parents", or perhaps a Gaelic year was longer in Morar!

They really were big, toughlooking lads, with hands like small shovels, and while they were somewhat overawed by us, we were certainly in fear of them.

Funerals

Talking of funerals puts me in mind of a few I remember. One in particular stands out.

Someone in the Railway Buildings had died; I don't know who it was, but I do remember being told about it by my mother, and that I was to be very quiet if I passed their door. Naturally, being curious, I went up to the house to have a look. A large number of men were outside the door, talking very quietly in loud whispers. They were all dressed in their Sunday best, but little black diamonds were sewn on to their sleeve.

I was put out a bit to see that all the windows were shut and the blinds drawn. I had hoped to see the soul coming out of the window on his way to heaven, but I was obviously too late. But I was given a very large biscuit and had a bite of it on my way home. When I came into the living room I was ordered outside, complete with biscuit, as funeral biscuits in the house would bring bad luck, and I had better go and give mine to the hens.

Women never attended funerals; they hid their grief in private. The coffin was mounted on poles and carried from the house by a relay of mourners to Morar cemetery. It was the practice for four men to carry the coffin, followed by the procession of mourners. Anyone meeting the cortège stopped and, with bowed head, waited for it to pass. There were resting-places along the roadside, consisting of large flat stones on which the coffin rested while the next team of four prepared to carry the remains to the next stop. Naturally, at each of the stops refreshments were served: the whisky bottles came out — carrying the dead was thirsty work.

On one Sunday walk my father pointed out the coffin rests to me and, although I was shown only two or three, he told me that he thought there were ten of them, spaced out over the two and a half miles to the graveyard. Although no comment was made by my father, I could clearly see the ends of the whisky bottles pushed in under the stone slabs. That was obviously the place of interment for dead whisky bottles.

The timing of the funeral was arranged so that the mourners, having watched the interment, could walk up to Morar Hotel by the station to have a dram or two while awaiting the arrival of the train to take them home to Mallaig. According to my mother, most of the men went to funerals to renew their acquaintance with the whisky bottle, rather than out of respect for the dead.

I seem to have completely diverged from my memories of the Morar trio, so I had better get back to that. When playtime came it was usual for us all to dash out into the yard — that is, with the exception of the Morar contingent. They went into the cookery room and sat down by their bikes to eat their piece. This didn't last very long, as they were shuffled out and made to join us in the yard.

Our pieces

At playtime it was the practice to go into the shelter to eat your piece. The piece was taken from home every morning, wrapped in the *Daily Record* or the *Oban Times*, and usually held together with a bit of knitting wool. As the seating accommodation was rather limited, we were usually obliged to squat down and lean against the wall. The piece was unwrapped and the top slice peeled open to examine the innards.

I usually had jam which had leached through and produced a glutinous mass which, when eaten, left only the jam to be licked off the paper before crumpling it up and throwing it away. The wind was the litter bin in Mallaig, and all litter was whipped up and ended in the sea.

We were always interested in what others had; most of the pieces were smeared with jam, but some had delicacies like condensed milk, H.P. sauce, cocoa powder, or even cheese.

Sometimes a piece could be swapped to make a change. One day I watched the lad next to me open up his piece to examine the contents. He turned to me and said: "Oh, hell, it's crowdie again. I hate the stuff!" "Why don't you ask your mother to put something different on for you?" I asked. "I can't do that, I have to do my own piece, you see!"

On another occasion a boy peeled off his top slice, exposing thin squares of dark chocolate. I told him he was lucky getting chocolate. His reply was: "This is no chocolate, it's slices of oxter tubes".

142

I had no idea what he meant and, when he offered me a bit, I declined. The only tubes I knew were bicycle tubes, and I was sure I wouldn't find those very palatable. I couldn't plead ignorance, however, as this would show a lack of understanding ending in my losing face. He said again: "Oxter tubes, that's my favourite". Brother Duncan enlightened me when I told him about it. He was able to tell me that this lad's elder brother was in his class and that he used to have *Oxo cubes* on his piece.

When the Morar boys first cycled to Mallaig school it took them nearly an hour because of the state of the road and having to push the bike up the hills. However, as they got wiser, they rode their bikes single file along the outside of the railway track and that way the journey only took twenty minutes. As I write this I am amazed that the education authority took such care in providing bicycles, especially in those days of extreme poverty in the crofting community.

Having seen the new bikes, Duncan and I pestered our mother to get one for us, telling her that some of the other boys in Duncan's class were getting one, but she wouldn't hear of it. Where would we use it? Either at the pier or round the station. My father condemned the whole idea. "They'll only go on the line with it, and I will not allow that."

About a year later the road from the village was made up and, with lorries and a steam roller the tarmac was laid down, right up to the top of Annie's Brae, about a third of the way to Morar. We were fascinated by the steam roller puffing backwards and forwards at two miles per hour.

The new road was the excuse to pester our mother again and, after a long time, she said she would buy us one between us. "But," she said, "mind you look after it, as it is costing nearly four pounds."

She was to get it from the catalogue. Duncan and I couldn't get down to the goods shed fast enough to collect it when we were told it had arrived. It was in a wooden crate and we had to carry it home and unpack it there. I was really thrilled; it was as nice as the Morar bikes and I was looking forward to having a spin on it. "You are not to get on it till your father gets home" came the command from Mother.

Father had a look at it and said: "If you go on the line with that thing I will put my boot through the wheel". Even now I believe he would have done.

I don't remember sharing it. Duncan was in full command and he reminded me that he had to write his name in the goods shed before we could take it out. Nevertheless, I was expected to clean it!

Soon after, most of the boys of our age had a new bike, and the new road from the station to the top of Annie's Brae became the cycle track.

CHAPTER
TWENTY-TWO

Sunday and Sunday School

It is impossible to write about school or school life without some mention of our Sunday School. I was a regular attender, not because I was particularly devout, but merely because there was nothing better to do.

In our household Sunday was the Sabbath Day, and both my parents were of the *Wee Free* persuasion, a minority group of the Free Church who had refused to merge with the United Presbyterian Church in 1900. We were not allowed to do anything that would conflict with their high ideals: this is the Sabbath Day and the Bible instructs us to keep it holy — only acts of holiness will be allowed.

We were permitted to eat our dinner, dress up for Sunday School and, if the weather was not too inclement, my parents would take me for an afternoon walk. I don't remember any other members of the family joining us; no doubt, as they were much older than I was, they were able to do holy things on their own!

In Mallaig all Sunday afternoon walkers used the railway line, but we always went on the road; no doubt my father, having walked the line all week, wanted to stretch his legs without being governed by the distance between the railway sleepers.

Dinner was prepared the day before and eaten at about two o'clock. As no-one got up very early on a Sunday, this was our first meal. When we had eaten, the table was cleared and the dirty dishes were stacked up in the scullery, unwashed until Monday.

Any youthful activity was frowned upon — no games of any kind were allowed; a pack of cards was the Devil's Bible and was always put out of sight on Saturday night. We were encouraged to read a school book or to revise some school lesson. These suggestions were ignored, and I usually asked if I could go and feed the hens. This was normally allowed, but "Mind you don't collect up any eggs!"

Should it be raining, and it usually was, I would kneel on the sofa and look out of the window over to the Isle of Skye; but there was nothing to see, as the boats were not permitted to enter or leave the harbour before midnight, and it was normally too misty to see much of Skye. My time was usually occupied by huffing on the window panes, and using my finger to practice my drawing in the condensed moisture. I was able to do this only once, as the window pane, now wet, would not lend itself to further adornment; I was now obliged to watch the rain drops on the outside of the pane running down and gaining impetus as they embraced the ones below, growing progressively in size.

I well remember my amazement when one of my sisters, I don't remember which one, admonished me with: "These windows are not for looking out of". I had never heard anything so daft, and told her so. I was quickly silenced when she elaborated and explained: "They are to let the light in!" I had never thought of that.

My parents usually attended church but always did so when there was a Gaelic service. My father seemed to me to spend the major part of a Sunday reading his Gaelic Bible; I sometimes wondered if he was checking up on the minister — or trying to find evidence that God was originally a Skyeman. At any rate I'm sure he *knew* that Gaelic was the first language in Heaven.

My mother normally spent her time reading, starting with the church magazine and finishing with the *People's Friend*. I do remember her breaching convention on occasions when, ignoring my father's glowering looks, she would take up her knitting or start darning my socks or jersey, or put a patch on my trousers.

She was a dab hand at the trouser patching — the patch could be of any colour or pattern and she did two stitches to the inch to have it all shipshape for school on Monday. Some days, on my way to school, I would tear the patches off, having learned that it was better to be ragged than ridiculed. Cries from the girls: "Is it Hallowe'en already?" made this despoiling of my mother's skill necessary. After all, I had my position to uphold!

There were two churches in the village; the smaller and older was the *Wee Free*. This was the church that served the indigenous inhabitants, and also the church that my parents attended. The newer church was the Church of Scotland. The nearest Roman Catholic church was in Arising, a village some seven miles away on the road to Fort William. Well do I remember the consternation in our household when it was announced that the Wee Free minister was to be transferred to a more populous area and that our church was to be incorporated into the Church of Scotland. (The word "transfer" was never used. It was replaced by "shift"."So-and-So has got a shift to . . ."; "they are shifting to . . .". Railway personnel seemed to be always shifting about).

The Wee Church was now known as the church hall and it was here that we assembled for Sunday School as usual. I don't remember my parents ever worshipping in the United Church of Scotland; some attendance was necessary — funerals, weddings and so on — but even I heard of fancy glass windows and pictures on the walls (so unlike the austere Wee Free and considered in our household as the first step to Roman Catholicism).

I stood at the church steps at most of the weddings, when the best man threw handfuls of pennies as the bride and groom made their way down the fourteen steps to the waiting bridal car on the road. I never made a fortune on the penny scramble as the older boys had bigger boots than I had. The skill was to place each foot over a pile of pennies and, without moving, to rake up the coins round about. When these were gathered up the foot was lifted, the coins collected and the trick repeated with the other foot.

Before leaving home to attend Sunday School we were given a penny to put in the plate. Everybody's penny had to be polished up and it was usual for us to leave home early in order to find a space by the roadside ditch and grub away in the mud and sand, busying ourselves burnishing our coins before presenting them to Jesus.

As we went into the church we were given a gummed paper stamp in exchange for our coin. The stamp proclaimed: "Jesus loves me", or "God is love", or even "Jesus saves". These platitudes were embossed on a floral background and we were required to lick the stamps and stick them on to our card. The card, when filled up, was our admission ticket to the Sunday School Picnic. At least, I think that was the bait. I know some of the boys had lost their card but nevertheless they managed to swell the numbers on the great day.

The Sunday School

Our Sunday School Superintendent was quite an elderly man. He was immaculately dressed in a blue navy jersey with the customary three pearl buttons on the neck band, navy blue trousers and, of course, highly polished boots. This outfit, set off by his white goatee beard, made him a very imposing figure to our eyes.

His name was Mr Acheson and he was part owner of a local fishing boat. We were told about the disciples being fishermen and that St Peter was their patron

149

saint. I think we looked upon him as St Peter himself; I know he gained our respect.

Sunday service usually started with: "Open your hymn book at hymn 116: All things bright and beautiful, all creatures great and small. We will omit verses 4 and 5".

The harmonium wheezed and off we went. Not that I took much part in the singing — as I previously said, I was never in very good voice, and I couldn't even follow the words as I had no idea what "omit" meant and quickly lost the place. Naturally pride would not allow me to enquire, but it didn't matter much in any case.

After the hymn we had prayers; the second line of the Lord's Prayer was "Harold be thy name" and any repetition of Mr Acheson's "Halleluia" was "Hardly knew ya".

The service finished with a psalm; no. 23 was favourite: "The Lord's my shepherd". The girls changed the words to those of Amazing Grace — Gracie MacLean was one of the older girls and this was obviously done at her instigation.

CHAPTER
TWENTY-THREE

The Sunday School Picnic

Our picnic always took place during the summer holidays and was a treat eagerly looked forward to. We travelled by train to Morar Sands, a journey of three miles and twenty minutes. The anticipation of the picnic and the lovely white sands — plus the hurl in the train — was all I could think of for weeks beforehand. But there was much more to it than this. It was customary for us to spend most of the summer in our bare feet, but as the impending great day drew near, my mother would say, "Go down to Davy's shop and get him to try on a pair of brown sandshoes — tell him you are for the Sunday School Picnic and that he is to book them out to me."

When we met at the station everybody seemed to be carrying something; some boys had footballs — real ones made of leather, complete with blown-up bladder inside — other boys had parts of herring boxes roughly hacked to resemble willow cricket bats. Instead of being autographed by Don Bradman or the like, the only writing, burned into the wood, read:

FISH, PERISHABLE

There were lots of small balls being kicked around while we waited for the train. The cricket balls were made of red sorba rubber and had a honeycombed construction. When struck by the hand they stotted all over the place and were very difficult to retrieve. This, of course, was all to the good, as it gave more time for the batsman to run between the sticks and so increase his score.

The girls had skipping ropes and all wore white sandshoes. Most of them had mouth organs; some girls played very well and provided us with entertainment during our long rail journey of twenty minutes. I knew some of the tunes at least, but I paid little attention to the *sook, sook, blaw* that the less experienced virtuosos seemed to favour.

Everyone on the platform seemed to be carrying something; there were half a dozen lady helpers all equipped with shopping bags, and clean herring boxes were filled with the essential goodies to make the picnic a success.

I felt rather odd, but, on reflection, I may well have been ill on the previous two Sundays and so I was not fully aware of what was required from me.

When we left the train at Morar station all our "luggage" was put out on to the platform and the two compartments which had been allocated to us had to be checked over to ensure that we had left nothing behind. We each had to carry something down to the shore: about two minutes' walk.

There was no flowing water in Mallaig, no river, not even a burn — all we had were the roadside ditches, so the river which flowed from Loch Morar was a great novelty for us.

Soon the sandshoes came off and were hung around our necks as the paddling began. As it was midsummer, the river flowing over the sand, although wide, was quite shallow and never reached our knees, but the pleasure of kicking clean water over your neighbour was a delight to savour; if you got soaked by him, this only added to the enjoyment.

Football

On one picnic I even took part in a game of football, but for once I was not the last to be picked as there were some smaller boys, even some girls were coaxed to join in, so that we could have two teams.

We played barefoot and, as a result, ours was a most sedate game. Try kicking a water-soaked leather football wearing only bare feet! Our team seemed to be called "Heid the ba" (head the ball), or at least when the ball came into our area this was the call that went up from our supporters, and as I was insufficiently skilled to head it, I preferred to adopt a stance of looking busy without being over-enthusiastic. I never knew what the score was and I don't think we had a referee.

The girls played skipping games, some individually, but the main event seemed to be two girls ca'ing a long rope and another jumping in at the correct moment. Other girls played peevers with the boxes drawn in the damp sand; they used chucky stones taken from the river and the game had to be modified somewhat, as the stones didn't slide on the sand when kicked and so they had to be thrown or rolled.

At last the long-awaited moment arrived. "Sit down on the rocks and we will have our picnic." (The sand was too damp.) The ladies came round carrying the herring box and we were each given a paper bag. Quickly opened, it revealed sandwiches, scones, pancakes and a little iced cake in frilly paper, a cake of chocolate and a poke of sweets.

We were then given a small bottle of either lemonade, kola or cream soda. We were not allowed to choose and I ended up with a bottle of fizzy kola. It was lovely; much better than our sugarallie water (of which more later). When all the empties had been collected our sandshoes were put back on and we were marched back to the station.

On the way back we sang:

"Is it pease brose again, Ma, pease brose again?
You feed me like a blackbird, and me your only wean."

Or the tattie-howkers' song:

"Some o' them had boots and stockings,
Some o' them had nane at a",
Some o' them had boots and stockings,
Coming up the Broomielaw."

154

Which referred to Irish families coming to Scotland to gather in the potato harvest.

When we arrived at the station all the boys rushed to go to the toilet. This was marked *Gentlemen*, and as the carriages had no corridor there were toilets at each station. We had a real good laugh at the cast-iron sign mounted on the inside of the modesty barrier: *Please adjust your dress before leaving.* As if boys or men wore dresses! Soon the train arrived and we rushed on board and found a seat, entertained all the way to Mallaig by the girls on the mouth organs.

When we got out of the train we had to carry all the empty bottles and paper bags back to the church and, needless to say, any unused bags containing consumable items were shared around.

As I dashed home to have my tea I wondered what it would be, but on opening the stair door I knew immediately. There was no need for a menu; the overpowering smell greeted me: *KIPPERS*. Ah, well!

My mother asked me if I had had a nice time and she instructed me to tell Mr Acheson what a good day we had had when I was next at Sunday School.

This was the last picnic I attended, as shortly after this my father got a shift to Crianlarich.

CHAPTER
TWENTY-FOUR

Holidays

It was not unusual for Duncan and myself to accompany both my parents to Fort William. I always found the train journey very exciting, especially as my father pointed out places of interest.

He explained in good time anything that he considered interesting and, as a result, my eyes were glued to the passing countryside while I waited for the object of interest to appear. He named all the stations that we were going to stop at, and he pointed out the hotels, all of which were built and run by the Railway. The inland salt water lochs along the shores of which we were travelling were also named and great emphasis was put on Glenfinnan viaduct, the first major concrete structure built in Britain. Soon we had to look out on the other side as Prince Charlie's monument came into view. It was sited at the head of the Loch and was reputed to be on the spot where the Highland chiefs and their men assembled to welcome the Young Pretender on his arrival from France.

Soon we crossed the swing bridge at Banavie over the Caledonian Canal. When the bridge was in the open position the road to Inverness and Mallaig was shut off.

(It is still in use today and, of course, the trains have priority.) When we arrived at Fort William station it appeared very dark and gloomy. Although it was usually raining in Mallaig, just as in Fort William, the Mallaig station had a glass roof and let through more light.

We trotted off to visit Auntie Maggie, my father's sister, who was married to Uncle Peter, also a railway employee. Their family was somewhat similar to ours; the eldest daughter, Maggie worked as a counter clerk in the Post Office. When Morag was directed to assist at Fort William, she stayed with them.

Memories of the family are vague, but I do remember them thanking my father for the box of kippers as we sat down to have our dinner. It was tatties and mince, and what really intrigued me was the cutlery. The knives and forks had bone handles, but the forks had only three prongs so, having mixed up my dinner, I enjoyed running my fork over it, making it into a lovely ploughed field with the furrows much further apart than I could make at home. The meal ended with the inevitable cup of tea, daintily served with saucers and accompanied by a teaspoon made of horn and wonderfully smooth. The tea was followed by scones and biscuits.

In the afternoon we played with my cousins while my parents had a look at the shops. Later, the eldest cousin took us back to the station, where we met up with my parents and Uncle Peter. Soon our train came in and we boarded it for our journey home.

Glasgow

Another family visit I remember was our trip to Glasgow. We travelled from Glasgow Queen Street station by tram car. The house my uncle (my father's brother) had was up a stair in a tenement.

The only incident I recall was going to bed and sleeping with my cousin, who was about my age and had very long fingernails. We must have had some sort of disagreement which ended up with me being severely clawed. I was unable to retaliate as among my many bad habits nail-biting was one of my pastimes. In the morning my body was severely scored and really painful but, when having a look in the scullery I came upon a piece of polished tin pierced by lots of nail holes, part of a shoe repair kit sold by Woolworth's. It was used to scarify the old sole before applying glue to attach a new rubber sole, supplied with the kit. This I took to bed with me that night and, without provocation, retaliated in no uncertain manner. In the end my sleeping companion got out of bed, while I went to sleep. I know who got the worse of the scratching encounter; I suppose his mother saw his wounds, but by that time we had left and it was never mentioned to me.

As I grew older and my mother had more time on her hands, the major part of the family having flown the nest, some time was given up to going on holiday. Rail travel was free and I think Mother took fair advantage of this privilege.

Berwick on Tweed

We visited Eyemouth and Burnmouth, the homes of my sisters-in-law, and I know that we stayed in Berwick on Tweed, but I don't know for how long. Jeannie's mother lived up a stair in a very narrow street marked Something-Wynd, and I know we had chips wrapped up in newspaper for supper. They were delicious and I think they were the first chips I had ever had. In Berwick on Tweed I remember noticing that one street leading from the square was called England Street and the street directly opposite was Scotland Street.

London

It was our London holiday that made the greatest impression on me. We had a taxi from King's Cross station to our accommodation in either Argyle Street or Square. The next day we went for a look round and, of course, got lost. Fortunately two policemen met up with us and, in answer to his enquiry, spoke to my father in Gaelic. It turned out that one of the policemen was from Skye and knew my father's family; they and he may even have been to school together, I don't know, but I got pretty fed up listening to them talking away in a foreign tongue while I had nothing better to do than watch the traffic passing, and hanging around quite bewildered with all the noise and bustle. Eventually we were given a police escort to our lodgings and I was very pleased that none of my school mates could see me now in the custody of two policemen.

CHAPTER
TWENTY-FIVE

Motor Transport

Given the poor state of the road some sixty years ago, it may appear strange that a chapter on motor transport should appear. Nevertheless, Mallaig boasted two second-hand lorries. They arrived on a platform truck and had started their journey in Glasgow. They had to wait in a siding for some weeks as no-one knew how to drive them on the roadway.

The larger and newer-looking one was a Fiat, equipped with solid tyres devoid of any tread. The second was a Ford. This one had wooden-spoked wheels but with pneumatic tyres. It also sported two lamps, complete with candle stubs. These were mounted on brackets similar to those on a bicycle, and, although designed to be detachable, they were now welded on by a heavy coating of rust. I remember I tried to get one off, even hammering it with a stone; but to no avail.

The Ford had the original half-doors fitted, but the doors for the Fiat had long since gone. Both vehicles had canvas roof covers, now very tatty, but patched up with a bit of boat's sail.

On wet days the roof bellied downwards and became a pond, which proved very useful when the windscreen got covered in seagull droppings. When these obscured the driver's view, he would push his fist into the bulge above his head, causing the water to cascade down over the screen, restoring it to its normal greasy state.

Refuelling

The petrol for the vehicles arrived in a large steel barrel which was rolled from the station up to the petrol pump, which was outside Davy's shop at the top of the first hill out from the village. Petrol was emptied into an underground tank and handpumped into two glass jars on the pump.

When petrol was wanted the hose was taken from the pump, and when the tap on the hose nozzle was turned, one jar would be emptied and half a gallon of petrol dispensed. If one gallon was required the tap on the nozzle was first shut and then reopened, allowing the other glass jar to empty.

On the Ford the petrol tank and the seat were one and the same and when the tank was being filled the sacking-covered cushion was taken off to expose the filler cap. This had a nail-like projection on the underside which was graduated to form the dipstick. Because of the inaccessibility of this device it was quite a common sight to see the Ford being pushed along the pier out of the way, after which the driver was obliged to siphon petrol from the Fiat to enable him to drive up to the petrol pump.

As a reward for helping to push we were sometimes encouraged to suck the rubber pipe, and although initially we swallowed some petrol, we eventually became quite adept at this, and, in the nature of such things, we in turn invited younger boys to follow our example, and we fair enjoyed laughing at them as they coughed and spluttered in an effort to get rid of the petrol they had swallowed.

On its journey up to the petrol pump the Ford was always driven backwards with the driver standing on the running board and steering and controlling the speed with the throttle lever. This was mounted under the steering wheel and the lever on the opposite side was marked "*Advance*" and "*Retard*". I accepted this backward refuelling procedure as normal until my brother Duncan explained the reason for this strange phenomenon.

The fuel was gravity-fed to the engine, and as there was little petrol in the tank, the engine would starve and stop; however, by turning the lorry around and pointing it down the hill, any remaining petrol would run down to the engine as the exit pipe was on the front of the tank. This was the reason the lorry had to reverse up Davy's Brae.

The lorries were mainly used to transport the herring to the kippering sheds, or to take fish up to the railway siding for loading on to the rail wagons.

Driving lessons

As the vehicles travelled mostly on railway property they had no number-plates, no road fund licence. I'm sure insurance was given no consideration.

As for the driver, once he managed to get it going, he was afraid to stop the engine, and the vehicles were often left unattended. When we came on such a tempting situation we were brave enough to climb up and sit on the seat and, making the appropriate noises and clutching the steering wheel, pretend to drive it.

When the driver returned, we would ask if we could stay in the lorry while he drove it. Usually we were lucky enough to be allowed and two of us would sit alongside the driver and watch his every movement.

The Fiat was the favourite lorry, even if it did have solid tyres and gave a very bumpy ride, especially when going along the wooden pier, but the main reason for our fondness for it was that in the evening it was left overnight on a slight hill overlooking the pier.

When we were older we would go down to the pier after our tea and, without trying to start the engine of the lorry, we would take the handbrake off and steer it down the slope onto the pier below.

This was the first phase of our driving test. Any other children around were allowed to go on the back to help us push the vehicle back to its parking place, so that next morning the driver wouldn't know we had moved it.

As we became more skilled, or perhaps more devious, we were able to start the beast up. We had to switch it on, pull this lever, press that pedal, put it into gear. When it was given a push from behind off we went down the slope with the engine running.

Of course there was a bit of panic and consternation to begin with, but as the pier below was pretty wide it didn't really matter if we did deviate a bit off course.

On reflection, I think we didn't steer it; we just aimed it clear of any fish boxes in our path. I am sure that anyone reading this will be amazed that children of twelve or thirteen managed to operate these levers in the correct order to start the engine. The reason we were able to do this was that if we saw the lorry stopped while being unloaded we would politely ask: "Can we have a hurl in your motor, mister?" Invariably he was so keen to show off his skill that our request was granted and two of us would sit alongside him, watching his every movement.

If he was in a good mood he would even answer our questions, provided of course, that he had no difficult action to perform, like turning the steering wheel. We would ask him what was this for or what did he have to do that for. Half the time the answer would be: "I'm not very sure myself, but that's how it has to be done".

When I asked him what the big knob on the floor was for he said: "That's for stopping the engine; it has to do with stopping the petrol". In reality this button was the ignition switch.

The Accident

But our driving experiences came to an ignominious conclusion.

On this particular evening it was my turn to drive the Fiat down the slope. It was a very wet night and the midges were out in force. However, I had no trouble in driving down on to the pier below, and turned the steering wheel hard over to the right in order to travel the length of the pier as was customary.

I had gained a fair old speed, at least four miles per hour, but instead of the lorry obeying the command from the steering wheel and turning right, it carried straight on, the pier being very slippery with discarded herring, fish guts and the heavy rain. All my passengers abandoned ship as they could see the inevitable happening, and with all the screaming and commotion going on I vainly tried to make the lorry follow the path I had expected it to go.

It appeared to me that there was nothing else I could do to prevent it going over the pier into the sea below.

I had one hope, however; the edge of the pier was built up with a balk of timber at least four to six inches high and, with a bit of luck, this would deflect the runaway, but in any case my best course of action was to get out as there was nothing more I could do. This I did and watched the poor old lorry sliding inexorably to its doom. It struck the balk of timber broadside on, teetered backwards and forwards, then, believe it or not, over it went, crashing into the sea below.

I don't know if the tide was high or low — however, fortunately there was no boat underneath. All that I wanted to do was to get out of the way, and my mates, who had joined me, were of a like opinion. We realised that this marked the end of our nocturnal driving lessons and, by mutual agreement, we beat it off home sharpish, after agreeing never to visit the pier ever again.

We were naturally very apprehensive about the whole affair, but we were too afraid to make any enquiries. Some two days later I overheard my two eldest brothers talking about it and how the railway crane had lifted it out of the water and it was now drying out.

The incident was treated very casually, as that very same night there had been a storm with terrific gusts of wind and a boat anchored in the bay had come adrift and was wrecked on the rocks on the opposite side of the bay. This was a locally owned fishing boat and had not been insured. It was of much greater interest than an old lorry blown off the pier.

The Fiat recovered

Years later when visiting Mallaig I enquired how the lorry had been salvaged. It turned out that it had landed on all four wheels and at low tide it was possible to attach a rope to it. A steel mesh net was then put down in front of it and at high tide a fishing boat pulled the lorry on to the net. The net, with the lorry on it, was dragged to a position below the steam crane, the corners of the net were shackled together and the lorry hoisted out and returned to dry land.

The crane and the steel net were used to lift anything heavy on to MacBrayne's boats for shipment to the Hebrides, including motor vehicles which had come in by rail. They were run off the rail trucks and on to the net which had been spread out on the pier, and the crane lifted the net up and deposited its contents on the deck of the ferry boat.

CHAPTER
TWENTY-SIX

Mallaig and the Railway

I must have been about thirteen when one of my chums left Mallaig. His father was the Customs and Excise officer and he had been transferred elsewhere. This ended our group, and my one remaining chum and I went our separate ways and were no longer a force to be reckoned with.

The signal box

Being alone was no fun and when I looked around for something better than school to interest or amuse me, I cultivated a friendship with a signalman with whom I had always been on good terms.

I spent most of my school-evading hours in the signal box, which was built high up about 200-300 yards from our house, overlooking the Sound of Sleat, giving a wonderful view of the Inner. The signalman was familiarly known as Roguie and was Sparks's elder brother. Because he worked shifts, I dodged either morning or afternoon school.

168

The signal box was spotless, the floor scrubbed daily, the stove black-leaded and shining like ebony; the levers and all the brass were given daily attention. The levers were never touched by hand but operated only when the signalman was holding a duster. This was to prevent any rust forming. The levers looked as though they had been chromium-plated and the contrast with Sparks's establishment was unbelievable.

I quickly learned all about signal boxes, and was even allowed to pull the levers; the red ones were for signals and the black ones for the points. I could operate the red ones but the black ones were much too hard for me to pull.

I later learned that as the points were a push-pull operation they were rod-operated, but the signals were pull only (returning by gravity) and cable-operated.

Locomotives

Locomotives were built at a large engine works, Cowlairs, outside Glasgow. It appeared to me that each new loco built had its maiden run pulling an empty passenger train to Mallaig. This section was one of the most demanding lengths of track, with steep gradients and really nasty curves, the latter making strict speed restrictions necessary, with the result that with the reduced speed the severe gradients were made even more difficult to overcome. This, coupled with the engine crew's unfamiliarity with the route sometimes meant the train had to run back downhill and wait until

169

maximum steam pressure was available before venturing forth once more. This must have been a common occurrence as these "specials" rarely arrived when expected.

All the special engines were designed for shipment to countries overseas and were usually painted in a shabby battleship-grey undercoat, but some were in full livery and I vividly remember seeing Canadian and Indian railway engines puffing their way into the station. All engines were very much bigger than we were accustomed to and were invariably equipped with a large search-light, a bell and a device on the funnel which I learned later was a spark arrester.

We had a very good view from our living-room windows as all the engines had to pass by our house on their way to the engine shed, before going on the turntable to be loaded up with coal and water in readiness for the return journey to Glasgow.

One very large monster was built for China (at least Alistair said so) and we looked on it with awe. It seemed particularly ugly and drab in its plain grey undercoat, and the whole male population turned out to see it. When the new reasonably-sized engines drove up to the turntable before starting to take the 2p.m. train back to Glasgow, the extra large ones could not be turned and returned tender first.

All these foreign engines had a very peculiar whistle, all different, and certainly different from our engines. The starting whistle from the station always continued for a much longer time than usual; no doubt the driver

170

of the exotic train wanted to show off his latest conquest.

My father was notified of the arrival of these new engines and was given a chart showing the weight, height and breadth of each one. All these measurements had to be checked, especially against the loading on the bridges, and when I saw him sally forth with his little hand trolley I knew we were to have a new arrival.

The trolley was of aluminium construction and had two adjustable flanged wheels. On top and across the two handles was a large clock-like instrument which registered the distance between the insides of the rails. There was also a very large spirit level to show that the rail camber on the curves was correct. My father pushed the trolley in front of him, like a pram, and I learned later that if any measurement was not within the specifications he pulled a lever, which discharged a yellow colour on to the track. This told his repair gang exactly where the fault was, and so if the distance between the rails was not the correct 4 ft. 8 ½ ins. or the camber was not within specification, the "Flying Gang" train was sent out to remedy the defects.

This train was based at Mallaig and under my father's control. It was made up of two passenger coaches, two flatbed trucks and about twenty men. It was equipped with jacks, levers and a general miscellany of rectifying equipment. The flatbed trucks carried sleepers, rails, chairs and, of course, lengths of rail that sat on top of the chairs, firmly held in position by a wooden wedge (ideal for fire-lighting at home, although this practice was frowned on by my father).

Some of the transient locomotives were designed to run on different rail widths: the Russian tracks were, I believe, almost 7 ft. wide and those engines, like the Chinese ones, had to be fitted with a temporary bogie to allow them to run on British tracks. This, of course, also raised the height, making the already huge engines even larger. The height of the overhead bridges was very critical, and even when they had been carefully checked by my father, the engine driver would pass under them at the slowest possible speed, having been told his freeboard was only two inches.

Traffic control

When a train left Mallaig, the next station on the route was notified by telephone; each signal box had a different Morse code call (Mallaig was one long, one short), but it was possible to listen in to any conversation.

The train was given a token at the signal box and this gave the driver a clear line for the section (about 15 miles). When the train arrived at the end of the section the token was exchanged for a differently-shaped one allowing him to go on to the next section. The first section was now cleared by the use of the token apparatus and so the Mallaig section could now send out the next train or, indeed, receive one.

Every train passing the box was logged with time and type and each entry ended with T.L.I.P. This was "Tail light in position", to show that the train had not broken apart.

The herring train

During the herring fishing season at least six fish specials left the village. These consisted of vans and were ice-packed to keep the fish in the best condition on their journey to Glasgow. I was very pleased to read on the side of each van:

FISH TRAFFIC — RETURN TO MALLAIG WHEN EMPTY

As there were not enough local crews or engines crews from other depots, complete with locomotives were imported, and it was quite a strange sight to see one engine pulling five or six unattended engines while the crews played cards in the coach which always brought up the rear.

The lamplighter

Sometimes, for a change, I would go round with the lamplighter. It was his job to look after and replenish the signal lamps. He had a can with a spout which he carried as he climbed the ladder, but when I was with him I did this job for him as I was more "soople" than he was, at least so he told me. The can contained not paraffin but rape oil. This oil was used in all railway lamps because it didn't char the wick and so, apart from a weekly fill-up, no maintenance was required.

The railway station

The railway station, too, afforded great pleasure. It was a glass-covered area, and in the evening most of the local men congregated below the railway clock to discuss daily events.

Perhaps at this stage I should make mention of time-keeping in the village. We had two times, the railway time and the wireless time and they were always at variance. This was the reason passengers always arrived at least half an hour too early. The older, pre-railway generation still used the simpler method: the boat came in in the morning, in the forenoon, at dinner time or after dinner. This was as accurate as was necessary.

In addition to the clock the station housed several red-painted vending machines. For one penny one could buy a cake (the term bar was never used) of Nestlé's chocolate, or one Churchman cigarette all nicely wrapped up in silver paper and in its own individual box, and the next machine gave a packet containing ten Sharps' caramels in exchange for the elusive penny.

The next machine printed out up to thirty letters on an aluminium strip. This machine had a manually operated pointer which was positioned to cover the letter or number on the face plate. A handle on the side was then operated, and on completion the name plate was delivered with neatly-rounded ends and two fixing holes. We were spoiled for choice! But the cigarette machine was the favourite, certainly in my age group.

During the day the station bustled with activity. The incoming passenger train was invaded by a host of cleaners, all the windows were shut and washed down, all the compartments swept clean, and any hot water cans emptied out, while men on top filled the water tanks for use in the toilets. Each coach was completely washed externally by the men cleaners, using long-handled special soft-hair sweeping brushes.

The hot water cans were foot-warmers and had to be booked in advance. These had a ridged top and looked not unlike a modern jerry can. They held about five gallons and they were collected at Crianlarich, about 100 miles south on the journey to Glasgow, where they were emptied and refilled if required or used for the return journey to Mallaig.

Alistair's duties

My eldest brother, Alistair, was an engine cleaner and, with two other mates, was on permanent night shift. Their duties included cleaning and polishing the locomotives, burnishing the buffers, oiling the external moving parts, and relighting the fire to get up steam.

When this was done, they drove the locomotive to the coal truck to replenish the coal in the tender. As if that was not enough, one of them had to wake up the driver and fireman on duty for the early morning train, which left at 6.35. He carried a long pole and would

175

tap on the window till the driver opened it. This was to ensure that he didn't go back to sleep. This was repeated at the signalman's house. During the herring season many more windows were tapped, as it was often necessary to make up a fish special train and this, of course, required a great deal of shunting. The first special would leave at about half past seven and they would continue frequently for the rest of the day.

Alistair was very railway-conscious and took his duties most seriously. This, in an era which demanded a twenty-year apprenticeship before one was permitted to be in charge of a locomotive. He was about forty-five before he held this exalted position, and only then at this early age because of the intervention of World War II and the increase in rail traffic. I must have been about seven or eight at the time, and I can say this with a degree of certainty as this was the time when I graduated from reading the comic *Bubbles* to the more advanced *Wizard* and *Hotspur*. Alistair bought them for me every week; not that I read them very much, but I did like the coloured pictures. I was able to make some sense of the story by reading the parts enclosed in the speech bubbles and ignoring the paragraph below each section, while I awaited Alistair's arrival.

As usual, I spent most of the day in bed. I must have been a very sickly child, and I clearly remember lying in bed and looking up at the ceiling with nothing better to do. I'm sure that this enforced absence from school contributed to the ease with which I was able to play truant; at any rate I do remember, on rejoining my class, being completely at a loss to understand, and it was quite impossible for me to catch up. As a result I naturally lost interest in the lessons, and my contribution was pulling faces behind the teacher's back as he wrote on the blackboard. The mirth that ensued was quickly stopped, as was the writing on the blackboard, and instead it was "get out your books and we will take turns at reading aloud". I didn't have a book and so I was excused.

I was certainly very bored lying in bed all day long, and I have since been told that I had every ailment a child was heir to (in fact I was led to believe that I had mumps and measles at the same time), and apart from being given my food and medicine, I was left pretty well to my own devices. Mother would attend periodically with cod liver oil and malt, which I was fond of. But this was followed by a white liquid labelled *Scott's Emulsion*; the trademark on the bottle was a fisherman holding up a very large fish whose tail was trailing on the ground. I hated the stuff, partly because the same spoon was used, and partly because I had to swallow the liquid, whereas I was generally allowed to suck the cod liver oil spoon, which tasted like liquid toffee, but never for very long, as the spoon was needed for the Scott's Emulsion. The medication sessions were usually accompanied by Mother's hand encompassing my brow, and often brought forth the words: "I'll put on a wee fire for you".

Mother was an expert at the firelighting but, of course, it was necessary to clean out the ashes left from the previous fire. She would come in, seconds later, armed with a pail and a shovel, and quickly cleared out the grate. All the ashes and unburned coal were transferred to the pail, ignoring any stour that her endeavours had displaced. Satisfied that the grate and pan were empty enough, she would march off with the pail and shovel, returning with a shovelful of glowing coal taken from the living-room fire and a pailful of coal for refuelling. The room was now enveloped in smoke, but providing not too much burning coal was upset and smouldering on the clootie rug, she was more than a match for that, and was very adept at stamping or shuffling on top of any smoking patches. As the smoke began to disperse, a shovelful of coal from the pail made it redouble its output, and at this point she left the room, well contented. Her parting shot was, "It will be a grand fire in a wee while."

Duncan visited me on one occasion immediately after the fire had been lit. He told me he could hear the spiders coughing for want of fresh air — as he was two years my senior I believed him, and although I listened very attentively, I was quite unable to hear them. When I told him this, he said that they had probably fainted or even died.

My greatest pleasure in my bedbound times was when Alistair came into the room with the two comics he had bought at the station bookstall. He read the stories to me and I really gloried in the exploits of the Wolf of Kabul, a tale about a British undercover agent who appeared to be winning the war in Afghanistan single-handed during the British invasion. That was in the *Wizard*, and the feature story in the *Hotspur* was the Black Sapper. He was able to travel underground in a boring machine, and to tunnel his way anywhere, to do the right thing and support the forces of law and order.

Alistair visited me most afternoons. Being an engine cleaner he was on permanent night shift and got up each day about one o'clock. I well remember his visits, as he would give me an extra spoonful of malt. After a time he tired of reading comics to me, and told me that he had applied for a job as a fireman.

This, of course, was promotion, and if he passed his oral exam he was on his way to becoming an engine driver. The exam worried him very much, and the Duties of the Fireman supplanted the comic reading.

For myself I have never driven a steam locomotive, in fact I was rarely allowed to stand on the hallowed footplate, but by the time leading up to Alistair's exam I am sure I knew more about the Duties of the Fireman than most engine drivers. I was not really interested in this topic, but as any company was better than none I felt obliged to show interest and be attentive. The Duties of the Fireman appeared to me to be so numerous that I found it difficult to know how he found time to throw the coal on to the fire.

The engine was collected at the engine shed, all coaled up and with the correct head of steam. The needle on the steam gauge must point between the two red lines. All the coal in the tender had to be washed to get rid of any dust, and any big lumps had to be broken up. The engine was then driven down to the platform to be filled up with water. No coal was to be put on the fire as the smoke would annoy any waiting passengers.

When the engine was coupled up to the waiting train, the fireman had to check all the hoses: brake hoses, steam hoses (for heating the carriages) and several more which I can't remember. He then had to go to the front to ensure that the lamp code was correct.

There were two lamps on each engine and their location on the brackets denoted the type of train (there were six brackets). These lamps were painted white and weren't lighted during the day time. I can't recall all the lamp code positions, but I do know that a Fish Special had one lamp only, high up on the smoke box, which gave the train priority over others because of its perishable freight.

Obviously Alistair was able to detect my lack of interest and, in an effort to spur me on, he asked me if there was anything I wanted to know about a "loco", as he called it. More to please him than to gain further knowledge, I asked if there was a clock in the cab. Now this was the biggest mistake I could have made. Clock, there was no need for any clock; every station had a clock that could be read from the engine, but a clock in the engine would very quickly be ruined by the vibration. There were, however, five dials, all in brass cases. These were polished every day by the cleaners, as were the copper pipes. The cleaning medium was soft soap and sand made into a paste and rubbed on in a piece of cotton waste. This waste was in plentiful supply and was made up of multi-coloured cotton strands. A clean piece of waste was used as the polishing cloth.

The regulator handle was similarly treated as the driver objected to getting his hand dirty.

The five dials were named in turn: the dial for steam pressure, another to tell how much water there was in the tender. The purpose and names of the other three I have forgotten. Alistair rattled off unfamiliar names at furious speed, leaving me impressed but confused. How was I expected to know what an injector was? I was clever enough not to enquire, as I knew this would prolong the session by at least half an hour. There was also a whistle code to be learned, and all signals and gradients had to be known.

When the train moved off, the cold air coming in chilled the fireman's back, while the heat from the glowing firebox scorched his knees. There was no protection against the elements, and on a wet day it was normal for him to be soaked on his back and scorched in front.

The roar of the engine made speech impossible and if the driver spoke to the fireman he could only nod and smile, pretending to understand. As the engine got up speed, it swayed from side to side and the footplate trembled under his feet in a dangerous manner. Laden with a shovelful of coal, the fireman had no support and nothing to hold on to as the locomotive jerked its way round the curves. (In Railway parlance corners were curves and hills gradients.)

The fire grate was enormous, and there were two separate fires: the main fire to generate enough heat for the steam, and the second, much smaller, fire which would be fired up when the main fire had been

181

clinkered up. When this happened, a heavy round iron bar, known as the "cleek", was pushed into the fire-grate and used to break up the clinkers before they were jammed into the fire bars.

A good fireman had the right colour of smoke coming out of the chimney; the smoke had to be grey in colour; black smoke meant that too much coal had been put on at one time and that there wasn't enough draught. White smoke meant too furious a fire and too much air. This type of fire would always open the safety valve and was a waste of time and effort. On a passenger train the fireman had to climb up on the coal tender and shovel the coal down to the opening in front. This could be done while the train was standing at the stations, but of course on a goods or fish special he was obliged to clamber up while the train was in motion, with nothing to hold onto and the tender swaying from side to side. This part of the job Alistair hated, as he was about twenty feet above the ground with only a shovel for support, and very unstable lumps of coal to stand on.

Alistair passed his fireman's test and his visits came to an end. I was really upset at this, but there were compensations. I recovered from my illness and there was much talk of Alistair's forthcoming marriage. He was to marry a fisher lass, and I don't think Mother was too pleased, but after the wedding she and Jeannie were very good friends. We saw very little of Alistair, and shortly afterwards he got a shift to Glasgow, not returning to Mallaig until after the war, and then as an engine driver.

CHAPTER
TWENTY-SEVEN

The Big Pier

There were two piers in Mallaig. The more substantial and very much larger one had the railway track running to the end of it, terminating in heavy buffers to prevent an overrun into the sea. This pier was primarily used by the ferry boats running to the Inner and Outer Hebrides.

These boats were operated by MacBrayne's and were the sole means of travel and transportation of goods to and from the islands. One side of the pier was used exclusively for this purpose. All goods came down from the station for shipment by means of goods vans, and a locomotive was always shunting in this area.

The other side of the pier was used for the coal trucks which carried the coal for the steam drifters. These were of iron construction with a single funnel and were engaged in fishing for any fish other than herring or mackerel.

There were so many drifters operating that each day a trainload of at least twelve coal trucks, each carrying 10 tons, arrived and was shunted down to the pier. The locomotive was at hand to position the trucks on to the discharge area, and move the empty wagon forward, and position a full truck above the waiting drifter below.

The coaling procedure was simple: the side door of the truck was unfastened, some coal fell out on to the track, and some fell on to the ship's deck. When the coal had stopped falling out and the dust had settled, a metal chute was fixed on to the truck and positioned over the edge of the pier to the waiting boat below. Coal was shovelled on to the chute until the truck was empty or until the boat had had its quota. The train was moved forward and presented the next full truck in position for discharge.

When all the trucks were emptied or when no more boats needed refuelling, the train was shunted back to the station, had any waiting fish wagons attached (after removal of any full coal wagons), a main line engine in front, and the train would leave on its journey south.

Coal which fell into the water was recovered by local men using home-made trawls. These were dragged along the sea bed by rowing boats. The washed coal was sold when the "colliers" returned to the wee pier and bought by locals and fisher girls for 2d. per pailful.

Coal

Coal appealed to me for some unknown reason, and when we had coal at home this was somewhat unusual and we eagerly watched as a coal wagon appeared on the railway in front of our house (at the same place as my mother had her hot water on washing-day) and a wooden rectangle was built into position, using hooks and eyes at the corners.

This rectangle had four sections, each about six feet long and perhaps three or four feet high. This box-like affair was filled with coal from the truck and levelled to the top.

The men from the Railway Buildings wheeled the coal to their houses; meanwhile the box was moved further on down the track to a new position. The coal truck was now manhandled to where the box was, and the procedure continued: the box and track were moved back to the first position and moved backwards and forwards until the truck was empty. Naturally my father took no part in this practical activity, but I know we were never short of coal.

There were nine railway cottages individually spaced along the line-side between Mallaig and Fort William. All were supplied with coal surreptitiously taken from the coal train stopping at all the cottages as required.

I know this as I overheard Alistair telling my father that he had had a day of it, what with shovelling the coal for the engine, and clambering out on the coal trucks, throwing out lumps of coal for Mrs So-and-So — complaining that he wasn't throwing it far enough — and she was getting it delivered all for nothing.

He did say, however, that she made a good cup of tea, and gave him and the driver a plateful of tattie scones. (Alistair was senior cleaner by now, and took over sometimes as relief fireman.) In view of all this I sometimes wonder if our coal fell off the back of a coal train!

Coal at cost price

I remember the amusement caused when a new Regional Engineer paid a visit to the Mallaig Line. Alistair told the tale. It appeared that the engineer felt very sorry for the surfacemen who lived isolated lives by the side of the railway. There was no roadway, and everything depended on the passing trains. He asked one woman what she used for heating and cooking, and, at her reply that she gathered wood to burn, he told her he would see if he could help. Sure enough, he arranged for a wagonload of coal to be shared among all the railway line-side cottages. This, he explained, would be at cost price — about £1 per ton. For the first time coal had to be paid for, and although the surfacemen couldn't refuse the kind offer, they declined any further delivery of coal and went back to their free fuel. They couldn't afford to buy coal.

The drifters

However, to get back to the pier: the drifters all came from the north or north-east coast but they fished for long periods each year from Mallaig. They fished in pairs with nets which were supported vertically with floating glass balls, the nets slung between them forming a screen in which the fish were enmeshed. The boats drifted with the tide during the operation, hence the name "drifter". The nets were of very strong construction and of large mesh as neither herring nor mackerel was caught by the boats.

186

When their catch was landed, this was laid out on the wee pier and auctioned boatload by boatload. The whole pier was covered with huge fish, and it was only possible to walk between the rows.

When the fish had been bought they were taken to the gutting benches where they were quickly gutted, put into boxes, and iced over to await collection by either the Ford or the Fiat and then taken up to the train standing at the station.

MacBrayne's had one paddle steamer, the *Glencoe*. She was used on the short Armadale (Skye)-Mallaig crossing. One day one of her paddle wheels struck an underwater obstruction as she was leaving the harbour. This paddle stopped, the ship slewed round on the one paddle and struck the pier, causing serious damage, and she was unable to sail again. The drive shaft had sheared and was beyond local repair. We were told this on the grapevine at school, but in addition that afternoon the diver was going down to see what she had hit.

Dinner time couldn't come quickly enough. I'm sure that most of the boys and girls in the class assembled at the pier without going home for dinner.

The diver

Sure enough, the diver's boat was out in the bay with four men on board. We arrived just in time to see the diver having his chest weights fitted. He then stood up and stepped into his lead-weighted boots, he next shuffled to the ladder which was hanging over the boat, where he was helped on to the top rung of the suspended ladder. He climbed slowly down trailing a hose pipe and a rope behind him.

Before he was completely submerged, a glass circle was screwed on to his bulbous helmet and when he gave a wave of his hand two of the men wound up the pump and the two big, iron wheels slowly revolved. The diver went on down the ladder, leaving great bubbles behind him.

The two wheels picked up speed and one of the girls suggested that they were trying to pump the water out of the harbour. She was quickly ridiculed, but not for long as the cry came up "the Master's coming!"

We quickly dodged through the assembled spectators back to school — just in time for the afternoon playtime. Apart from the belated register being called, nothing was said about our absence until the headmaster came in. He lectured us on our folly and pointed out the dangers; if only we had told him about the diver he would have taken us down in an orderly fashion, as this sort of incident had a great deal of educational value. However, now we must be punished and when time permitted we would be kept in after school to write a composition about it. We never did — he must have forgotten about it — but anyway we knew he would never have marched us down to the pier, and we felt very pleased with ourselves at having escaped punishment.

Even now it seems strange that a village as small as Mallaig should have a deep sea diver with all the necessary equipment. I now know that part of his duties was to examine all the piers in the Island for underwater erosion. Most of them were built on wooden piles. In addition he would fit new propellers to boats which had had them damaged or lost, and he also attended to propellers which had become entangled with ropes or netting.

The diver's son was in Duncan's class and answered to the name "Sgarbh", which I believe is the Gaelic for cormorant; very apt, I think now.

The obstruction on the seabed was a heavy metal trawl which had obviously fallen overboard from one of the drifters.

The trawl was subsequently winched up to the pier, but the poor old "*Glencoe*" was ignominiously towed away and never came back on the Mallaig to Skye line.

The *Dunara Castle*

While MacBrayne had the monopoly for the conveyance of passengers and light goods, all livestock and heavy freight, including coal, bags of oatmeal and flour were carried by another company, which appeared to have only two cargo ships; at least only two called in at Mallaig. The larger of the two, the "*Dunara Castle*", called in quite frequently, usually to discharge sheep from the islands for sale on the mainland.

When she berthed, it was very exciting for us children, as the sheep had to travel from the big pier to the loading pens, a journey of about a quarter of a mile, to await forward shipment by rail.

When the animals were discharged from the cargo boat they were naturally very frisky, having been penned up for two days, and on route to the pens men and boys were positioned at strategic points to prevent the sheep making their way down to the wee pier, into the station, or into the village shopping area.

Soon the whole area was covered with sheep, all bleating away and apparently determined to disoblige the men who were shooing them on; the sheep would much rather evade the guards and run into the village. This presented quite a problem as if and when it happened with one sheep, the rest of the flock followed, and as the guard could not leave his post it was up to us children to chase after the recalcitrant animals and return them to the main flock — all good clean fun. Eventually all the sheep were enclosed in the wooden pens until such time as the cattle trucks were positioned. In some cases the sheep stayed overnight in the pens, and although water was available in the troughs, I cannot remember them having anything to eat.

The sawdust shed

Close to the pens stood the sawdust shed. This was quite a large wooden building and usually half full of nice dry sawdust, which was wheeled out on a barrow and spread on the floor of the trucks before the sheep were driven in.

As children we found this the ideal place to go, especially on a wet day. We found the key under the stone by the door, and, as the shed had no window, the stone was used to keep the door partially open. Here we played in the sawdust, built roads and army trenches, and, by using the barrow and a large square-mouthed shovel, all kinds of intricate designs were made. We even had a church interior with pulpit and pews. As there was no sand on the village foreshore, the sawdust made an admirable substitute.

As we grew older and remained undetected the shed took on a more noble character; it became the Smoking Room.

First, cigarettes and matches had to be to hand, a place of concealment had to be found, and, as no pleasure was to be had in smoking alone, a mate with a like mind had to be found.

No pleasure was to be had if one tried to smoke in the dark, so some form of light was necessary (the reader may recall that the tail lamp from the train was used for smoking when we were in our home-made hut).

If we had only one cigarette, that is, a Churchman from the station machine, the cigarette was cut into two parts, and although this meant throwing away two ends, much more pleasure was derived from smoking together, rather than from the "one puff each" method.

About this time a Woodbine cigarette machine appeared outside Wee Archie's shop. On insertion of two pennies a packet of five cigarettes dropped down. This was ideal as we could now have a whole fag each. The complication was, however, how to conceal the half-empty packet — we dared not take it home.

Sometimes younger boys would visit us when we were smoking in the sawdust shed and we would delight them by showing off, making the smoke come out of our nose. This really filled them with wonder, until my mate Jerry explained that he could make the smoke come out of his ears. Would they like to see him do this?

Knowing what was to follow, I was rather sorry at their eagerness when he explained that one of the boys must help him. The largest boy volunteered and Jerry told him he had to stand in front and push the palm of his hand on to Jerry's stomach while looking up at the emission of smoke from the ears.

When the stage was set, Jerry took a puff at his Woodbine, casually took the fag out of his mouth and dropped his arm down, "accidentally" brushing the red hot tip over the back of the wee fellow's hand. In the howling and confusion that followed, Jerry said, "Did ye no' see it — the smoke was fair belting out of both my ears. Well, you'll have to look better next time." Naturally, there never was a next time, while most of the lads were gathered around, consoling the injured boy. One or two of the youngsters did say they saw the smoke coming out of Jerry's ears.

The horse

My final word regarding the Big Pier must be about the horse. There were no horses ever to be seen in the village, as very little agricultural land was to be had and

192

any crofting was done using the cas-chrom, or foot plough.

So when we learned (I don't remember how) that there was a big horse at the cattle pens, Jerry and I just had to see it, even if it did mean giving ourselves yet another half day's holiday.

After going home for dinner, I joined up with my chum and off we set to see this animal. It was huge, I might even say colossal: a great big black and white dappled Clydesdale with heavily feathered fetlocks and shoes as big as frying-pans — at least that's what the imprint in the mud showed. We had learnt something about the size of elephants and whales at school but this was bigger by far than anything we had imagined.

We heard that it was to go on the *Dunara Castle* for shipment to the Outer Hebrides, and this, of course, necessitated a trip down to the Big Pier. I was surprised how docile the animal was when a rope was put around its neck and "groom" and horse moved off. On arrival at the pier the horse-box was in position and the horse was encouraged to enter.

The horse-box was of proper construction and used for putting cows and bulls on to the boat; it had a door each end and both doors were opened when the animal went in but both were slammed shut when it was safely inside. There were semi-circular iron rods on top above the box. These allowed the animal to see out but prevented any attempt to escape.

The horse was guided forwards to enter the box, but it was so tall that its head struck the iron hoops and so it quickly backed away. Several men tried to coax and push the animal forward but to no avail — the horse kept going backwards and soon scattered all the well-meaning assistants. It was only by hitching the rope round a bollard that the frightened beast was prevented from backing off and over the pier. A confab now followed.

Although we were very interested, we were too frightened to go too near and we could only stand and watch developments without being able to hear. Soon two of the men went off and returned with a belly sling. This was laid out and examined and pulled about by the men with much head-shaking. It was obvious to us that this was not approved. However, minutes later a second sling was produced and put on top of the first one; obviously two slings were to be used. The men now returned to the horse and made great efforts to get the animal up to where the slings were. The horse didn't agree with this and despite a lot of pulling and pushing wouldn't budge.

I heard one man say: "Now, watch out, Donald, he can be dangerous at both ends". So, if the mountain wouldn't come to Mohammed . . . the slings had to be dragged down to the horse and pulled between its legs, lashed with ropes over the animal's back and securely knotted.

The steam crane was now called for and, with jib fully extended, advanced slowly along the railway line, stopping with the jib poised directly above the package. Down came the hook and it was attached. The man in charge waved his hand in a slow circular action and the flywheel mounted outside the cab started to revolve.

Nothing seemed to happen until suddenly the animal was suspended on the end of the wire rope. The horse was actually screaming and all four hooves were thrashing about in the air, the animal was swinging about as it went round and round, the long jib of the crane bouncing up and down.

Jerry and I were off! We sought refuge in an empty coal wagon nearby, having assured ourselves that when the horse landed back on the pier, as we were sure it must, it couldn't catch us.

The poor horse was about three feet up in the air when the crane began its slow journey back to where the *Dunara Castle* waited, the jib still bouncing up and down in response to the frenzied actions of its load. The animal was kept suspended until it had exhausted itself and its struggles had all but stopped. The crane's jib was then slewed until it was directly above the boat when it was slowly lowered until the animal disappeared below the edge of the pier.

I was late in getting home and was greeted by my mother, "Kept in after school again, I suppose". I have since wondered how the horse was unshipped when it reached its destination, but I have now learned the method. The animal was tossed overboard between the local ferry boat and the cargo boat, the latter being as near to the shore as was possible. The crew of the ferry boat picked up the end of the rope, which was around the animal's neck, and the swimming horse was piloted to the jetty.

CHAPTER
TWENTY-EIGHT

Herring Fishing and the Wee Pier

In my day Mallaig was the largest herring fishing port in Europe. During the summer months the Wee Pier was a seething mass of fisherfolk, both male and female, the latter being the majority by far.

Herring are migratory fish and travelled in vast shoals from the south-west Ayrshire coast up the north-west coast and seemed to me to end at Aberdeen. Not only were the fish migratory but the people whose livelihood depended upon them were in turn obliged to follow the fish around.

My second eldest brother, Roddy, was included in this annual trek and left home to go to Girvan at the beginning of each season, arriving back home in August or September.

As many as forty boats fished out of Mallaig during the season, which was from early June until September. Each boat arriving with its catch was accompanied by a retinue of gulls, and what with the creaking of derricks, the shrieking of gulls and the shouting of the men,

196

watching the uploading process was impossible except for a very short time.

As the catch was being unloaded the boat had to be refuelled and, of course, reprovisioned. Usually the boats were at sea for two nights, arriving back at the pier as early as possible in order to be first in the queue to have their catch auctioned.

The unit of measurement for fish is the cran, which represents four basketfuls and is a unit of capacity rather than weight — about 35 gallons.

As the unloading took place, the baskets were emptied into wooden tubs called kits. About twelve of these kits mounted on four-wheeled trolleys stood on the pier above the boat. Each kit held one cran and when the trolley was filled it was pushed or pulled along the pier to the gutting area at the shore end. Here the kits were emptied into very large open rectangular vats; there were at least ten of them, each about twice the size of a billiard table.

On three sides of the vats, evenly spaced out, stood the girls who were employed to gut the herring. They stood on upturned fish-boxes and were equipped with rubber boots, a rubber apron and, of course, an evil-looking, very sharp-pointed knife. The tips of the girls' fingers were bandaged, not because they had been cut but to prevent them from being cut.

The gutting process was simple: the herring was held in the left hand, the knife inserted at the throat, given half a turn, withdrawn, and the herring thrown behind to land unerringly in an open-topped barrel as the guts slid down the apron into a container below. As the barrels filled up, the herring were packed in layers by the man in charge of the vat, who added a scoopful of salt between each layer. When each barrel was filled, the top was put on and the addition of the iron hoop completed the task. When a replacement empty barrel was in position, the filled one was rolled away to join hundreds of others at the far end of the pier. On reflection I am quite sure that the girls must have been paid by results as not a single second was wasted.

Once each year boats from the eastern European countries would arrive to collect the barrels of salt herring. These boats were not allowed to dock but were required to wait outside the three-mile limit until the barrels were ferried out to them by local fisher boats.

Most of the schoolboys helped to roll the barrels from the barrel park to the local boat waiting at the pier, and it was usual for us to be given sixpence each — wages indeed.

However, the greatest treat was to be allowed out with the barrels to see the klondikers. This pleasure was denied me but I heard all about the Russian and Polish boats (bigger by far than any of MacBrayne's steamers) from boys whose fathers worked on the "ferry" boats and who were allowed to accompany their fathers out to sea.

An open barrel of salt herring stood outside each of the grocery shops in the village and customers scooped the herring out with the ladle attached to the barrel.

The ladle had holes in it to allow the brine to run out. Hundreds of barrels were shipped out to the Islands on MacBrayne's boats as tatties and herring were the staple diet of the crofters.

Truckloads of salt herring were transported to the Channel ports en route to Germany and Holland and fresh herring, boxed and packed in ice, made up at least one trainload every day.

It was quite usual for more herring to be landed than could be processed and it was customary for the surplus to be dumped into empty coal trucks, sheeted over with tarpaulins and shipped off to be processed into fish meal. Each railway truck was labelled BULK HERRING — URGENT. I have seen as many as two trainloads of bulk herring, each consisting of 10–15 trucks, leaving every day.

When the market was saturated, the luckless boats had to go back to sea and dump their entire catch overboard.

The gulls

The wooden pier was awash with squashed herring (run over by the trucks) and, of course, any herring dropped out of over-filled baskets, so much so that the gulls had difficulty in eating them all.

In any case the gulls seemed to prefer eating the spent herring that we threw up in the air. The fish was swallowed whole but always head-first. I can't remember a fish landing back on the pier uncaught by the voracious birds overhead.

Duncan told me of a little ploy he and his mates had got up to the previous year. Two herring were filleted but the head was left on one of each of the fillets. The two fillets with the heads on were put together with one head at each end and a piece of wood pulled through them to join them together with some six inches protruding from each side. This arrangement prevented the herring being swallowed.

The two-headed herring was thrown up and immediately caught and swallowed by one gull right up to the stick. The remaining herring head still exposed was quickly swallowed by another gull and both gulls were now beak to beak, fighting to gain possession. Eventually the gulls landed on the pier and the herring broke in two. Seconds later only the stick was left. We thought we would try this for ourselves next year but we never got round to it.

The Billiard Room

My evening entertainment and sporting activities were now focused on the Billiard Room. Actually, there were two billiard rooms in the village, but children of our age were not allowed in one.

The Billiard Room which I frequented had two tables, and there was a very large coal-burning stove at one end. Seating was provided around the hall, and with the companionship and a lovely warm fire it was the ideal place to be. Billiards was the favourite game with snooker a poor second. The hall was usually crowded with fishermen from the boats, and the tables were in great demand.

Although I was rarely allowed to play, I quickly learned all the rules, and on occasion I marked up the scores on the scoreboard mounted on the wall. This was an important job as neither of the players was permitted to alter the scoreboard.

Card games were also played — pontoon was the favourite — with the stakes in pennies.

There was also a kiosk selling chocolates and cigarettes. It was at this time that Mars bars made their first appearance and they were very popular at a penny each. I was often rewarded with one by the winner after an important billiards match.

Mr Wolfe

Strange as it may seem, we also had a resident packman in the village. Mr Wolfe was a Jew and his facial features, particularly his large nose, confirmed this. He was well-accepted in the village and I can see him now, opening up his pack, containing drapery or millinery in gay colours, on the floor of our house. The pack cover was made of brown rexine, and when in transit Mr Wolfe carried it by putting his arm through its leather straps.

He was often to be seen traipsing through the village with his very large pack and we children, strange to say, never made fun of him. He was a very keen billiard player, but invariably lost, and, as a consequence, he was obliged to pay for the table, as the rule was that the loser paid.

The funeral coach

He died shortly before we left Mallaig, and this was the only time I saw the funeral coach used to carry a coffin out of the village. The funeral coach was a special railway carriage, part van and part coach, consisting of three compartments for the mourners and the van for the coffin. The exterior was a very dark brown but the door handles were highly-polished brass.

It was not unusual for the funeral coach to come into Mallaig and the coffin to be transferred to the steamer for shipment to Skye or the Outer Hebrides, but this was the first time I had seen it leave Mallaig. I believe several male Jews came to arrange the funeral and they went back on the coach, which was the first coach (behind the engine) when the afternoon passenger train left.

The fisher lasses

As far as I was concerned the imminent arrival of the herring season most vivid in my mind was occasioned by Roguie, the signalman, arriving for his shift in the signal box, and entering singing:

The lassies are coming, hurray, hurray,
We'll see them the morn, but no' the day.

I'll go for my pleasure, whit mair can I say,
It'll no' cost a penny, there's naething to pay.

The continuation of this doggerel would put William McGonagall to shame, but this was more or less as I remember the first verse. The song gained in bawdiness as it went on and was accompanied by Roguie's performance of the highland fling. When he calmed down he told his mate that they were sorting the huts at the Point in readiness for the arrival of the fisher lassies "the morn's morn".

The huts were built on the promontory which formed one arm of the bay and they were used only by the itinerant fisher lasses during their stay in Mallaig. There were about twenty to thirty huts and, although empty most of the year, they were well looked after and maintained in a good state of repair. Some of them even had a small garden in front.

We, as children, were not encouraged to go there, but according to Roguie much better fun was to be found there than in the Billiard Room. I recall going down there but the only fun we had was putting our finger over the standpipes and squirting the water over each other or anyone else who passed.

In the middle of the complex stood the communal toilet; we went in there once (during the off-season, of course). The toilets were of sheet-iron construction and with open tops, except directly over the doorless cubicles which were enclosed. There were ten or more such cubicles, each of which had a fixed wooden seat mounted directly above a watercourse, always filled with running water.

I remember telling Duncan about our visit and he honoured (or humoured) me by telling me of one of the ploys in which he had taken part in earlier years. Apparently he and his mates had dipped a wad of cotton waste into some paraffin (both very common around engine sheds), had taken it along to the toilet block and, having set it alight, dropped it into the waterway, from the outside, of course. His gang had had great fun watching the lasses running out in varying states of *déshabillé* and screaming at the tops of their voices as the fire moved along the waterway. This trick could not be repeated as a frame of wire netting had since been set in position before the first toilet, filtering out any foreign solids which might be put in the waterway.

When occupied, the hutted area resulted in a compact and tidy community and the huts, neatly painted, were probably the forerunners of the post-war prefabs.

The lasses were readily identifiable; they were always neatly dressed in black and white and were never seen alone in the village. They spoke a language completely foreign to us, "broad Scotch" and they seemed to be always talking while going about, but what about we never knew.

Marriages

The arrival of the girls was greeted by the local boys as a pleasure sent from heaven, and very many girls married local boys, including my two eldest brothers, both of whom married fisher lasses.

Alistair's wife came from Eyemouth, a fishing village on the east coast on the Scottish/English border, Roddy's wife from the neighbouring village of Burnmouth.

The girls were not over-friendly towards each other and I later learned that there was a fair degree of jealousy between the two fishing villages. Although both girls were very kind to me, I had great difficulty in talking to them as their language and accent were quite beyond my understanding.

Most of the girls who married local boys, stayed in Mallaig and this was why there was the third stratum in Mallaig society.

I well remember Alistair's wedding. I must have been about thirteen at the time. The reception was held in the village hall and I recall the beanfeast we had: long tables, white tablecloths, tables laden with cakes and scones, as much as you could eat.

There seemed to be a wedding reception once a week, and we hungry kids tried to sneak in and help to dispose of even the left-over cakes which were neatly piled up in the cloakroom.

When the happy couple left to go on honeymoon, it was customary to have fog signals fixed on to the rails. These were detonated by the train as it left the station and they made a very loud report. The number of these detonators seemed to be in proportion to the popularity of the groom and varied between five and ten.

The Railway authorities must have thought Mallaig was continually enveloped in fog as the number expended was out of all proportion to climatic conditions — even for the West Highlands. The fog signals were painted red and were the size of a small tea biscuit but with a radiused top. Each had two lead tapes which were twisted round the rail to hold it in position.

Duncan collected the tapes and was quite expert at cutting moulds in a potato. He poured the molten lead which was heated at the engine shed and I remember sporting a lead anchor which he made; it was very presentable and when new was very shiny and, to my mind, not unlike silver.

On reflection and in my old age, it has occurred to me that the term "shot-gun wedding" must have had its origins in Mallaig. The marriage was normally one of compulsion, rather than of love or affection, with a shot-gun effect created by the loud reports of the fog signals. What could have better summed up the weekly event?

Unwanted pregnancies were only too common in Mallaig and a shot-gun wedding only resulted if the prospective mother was lucky. If, on the other hand, her claim was not accepted by the accused "father", and no wedding was to take place, then this was a matter for the Magistrate's Court in Fort William. According to my mentor, no such claim had ever been upheld. The girl usually had one or two girlfriends who swore that there had been an association, but the boy had brought along about six of his friends who swore that they, too, had on several occasions enjoyed the plaintiff's nocturnal company. The chairman of the bench was reputed to have said: "If you fall into a bunch of nettles it is difficult to know which one stung you!" Another girl claimed an elderly widower, stating in her evidence that she knew he was the father of her child, as the baby had been born without any teeth, just like him.

According to Roguie, however, Beecham's Powders, taken with a glass of whisky, could cure an unwanted pregnancy. In my youthful ignorance I assumed that the cure would need to be taken by the female member of the union, and although many men were "claimed" (called into question), Roguie, thanks to his intimate knowledge of and belief in the efficaciousness of the remedy, was never claimed, unlike almost all the other eligible men of the village. Roguie was fully aware that he might be claimed and, to ensure against a contingency such as fathering twins (which, he said, ran in his family), he doubled the dose, as he would say: "You never know what might happen, and in any case a Johnny Walker's Black Label is a very palatable medicine and I've quite got to like it".

CHAPTER
TWENTY-NINE

The Age of Steam

When I look back on it, it appears to me that Mallaig was constantly enveloped in a blanket of smoke. During the day the shunting engine was in continual motion, moving coal trucks around and making up the empty wagons into some sort of order for the return journey, and of course the herring trucks had to be hitched on at the back to make up the train. It was necessary for the engine to puff out its quota of smoke into the atmosphere.

This, of course, was added to by MacBrayne's steamers, which, in turn, encouraged the steam drifters to compete, and of course, all houses were dependent on coal fires for cooking and heating, which added to the daily haze.

To a lesser extent every male in the village from the age of ten or eleven made his contribution: the mature men stoked up their pipes with bogey roll tobacco. This was a tarry, rope-like substance and was kept in a tin in the waistcoat pocket. It had to be thinly sliced up with a very sharp knife; the slices were rolled up in the palms of the hands before being tamped into the pipe bowl. When the pipe was ignited and drawing well, clouds of foul-smelling smoke were emitted. The younger men smoked Capstan or Woodbine cigarettes; the younger schoolboys, the eleven-to-fourteens, helped with their fags or fag ends.

Some of us showed off that we could swallow the smoke, others were celebrating the passing of the Qualifying Exam but the majority were commiserating with each other on their lack of success.

All trains coming into Mallaig gave off very little smoke as the last two or three miles were downhill to sea level, but by Jove, they made up for it on their journey out!

For the return journey two engines yoked together came down from the engine shed (one had to be put on the turntable as it had taken the last train in); both stopped at the end of the platform where the two water columns were.

The fireman unhooked the pigskin hose, a huge, overgrown bag-like thing, and the "bag" was offered up to the driver who was on the top of the coal on the tender. The hose was pushed into the now open water tank, the fireman turned the water column wheel, and the bag took on an oval shape as the water rushed up to the engine's tank.

There seemed to be no indicator showing the contents of the tank, and as the tank overflowed water cascaded over the engine platform, and, if the hose had not been pushed in far enough, it jumped out, and the engine driver (who had been waiting to put the circular cover back on the tank) had a cold-water shower whilst "sprackling" over the coal shouting "Pit it aff, pit it aff!"

as he rushed off to his warm cab, shaking the water off his dungarees and cursing at the top of his voice at the ineptitude of his mate.

This was the bit we loved best of all! If we had nothing better to do we would go to the water column and ask the fireman questions about his engine, thereby diverting him from his duties, hoping that we would hear the driver cry out: "Pit it aff!" as the tank overflowed. This ploy was naturally known to us as "come on, we'll go and have a look at *PIT IT AFF*".

The engines, in tandem, now backed slowly along the platform where they gently met up with the buffers of the waiting train. The guard appeared and he jumped down from the platform and hitched the engine's coupling on to the train, the screw was turned up to tighten the links, thereby holding the buffers tightly together, and allowing no play between engine and coaches, making for a more comfortable journey.

Up front the two engine fires were being refuelled, although there was already a full head of steam — the safety valve was open and pumping steam over the whole station, and, of course, clouds of black smoke were belching out of both chimneys. The driver had turned on the sand valve and sand poured down a tube in front of the driving wheels. When all was ready, and the starting signal pulled down, it was time for take-off.

Doors were slammed, the guard blew his whistle and waved his flag; the engines responded with a real good "toot", great gouts of smoke came out of the chimney, and although the huge driving wheels raced frantically round, the train didn't move but remained at the

210

platform. More sand was pumped down on to the rails in front of both engine's wheels in a supreme effort to provide maximum traction.

At least ten puffs of smoke were required before the driving wheels stopped their frantic revolutions, and slowly it was "puff-puff" as the driving wheels, helped by the additional sand, gained the necessary traction to move the whole train, complete with two or three vanloads of kippers at the rear, away from the platform.

As the train passed the signal box on its way to Fort William each engine gave a "toot-toot" on its whistle. I never knew if this was to praise the docile monsters under the engine drivers' control or for them to congratulate each other on their success. However, they were probably saying "hello" to Roguie or to one of the other signalmen on duty.

It was not unusual for the interval between the "puff-puff" at the station and the "toot-toot" at the signal box to be interrupted by "bang, bang!" from the fog signals on the line, if there had been a wedding that day.

The last train left the village at 2.30 and from then until teatime the atmosphere was reasonably clear, and it was possible to see the Inner Islands once again.

There was no smoke abatement society or concern about the ozone layer in those days!

CHAPTER
THIRTY

Kippering

Only the best of the herring was used for kippering and so naturally commanded a much better price than those sold as fresh or salt herring. Mallaig herring were renowned as the best kippers available, and were always in great demand; this was particularly true in the village, where every household had at least one weekly meal of the delicacy — everyone knew someone who knew someone else who could let them have a pair each week during the season.

There were at least twelve kippering kilns, all sited at or near the Big Pier. My brother Roddy was foreman at the largest kiln; he latterly became manager and, having married his kippering lass from Burnmouth, settled down in the village.

The kippering girls thought themselves superior to the gutters, who mostly came from Eyemouth, and were not quite so "refined". In any case, gutters had to work outside in all weathers, while the kipperers were always under cover and in the dry; they even sat down — on very long benches upholstered with hessian sacks.

When a container was filled with gutted herring, it was dragged to the pickling vat, where the fish was pickled and dyed. The dye came in a round, metal drum, and my brother was responsible for mixing the dye powder into the tank before adding the saline solution to the pickling vat. His hands and arms were the colour of rusty iron up to his elbows, and, although he wore a rubber apron, even his chest was usually speckled. The drums were marked *DFK* and when I asked Roddy what this stood for, he fobbed me off with: "*Dye For Kippers*, of course!" I never did find out what the letters represented.

After several hours' immersion in the pickle vats the kippers were hung on wooden poles, known to us as "tender" poles; they had hooks on the sides to support the herring. The girls hung the fish on the rods, twenty fish each side; a gap without hooks was left in the middle so that the smoker could carry a rod in each hand as he climbed up the ladder in the kiln.

The smoker was a very important person and he enjoyed semi-professional status, almost on a par with the buyer. Both of them appeared part of a team, travelling around following the herrings' migration. I remember hearing Roddy's smoker telling him: "I'm here to smoke the fush, not to cook them!"

Herring smoking took place only in the late afternoon, the fires having been prepared beforehand. They were made up of wooden chips in little heaps on the floor, and a large container of oak sawdust was to hand. The smoker and his two helpers spent the early afternoon running up the ladder inside the kiln with the rods full of herring, one in each hand, returning empty-handed to collect the next load. The ladder inside the kiln had no protective sides, and the impetus of gaining a speedy foothold on the first rung seemed necessary to maintain the balance.

Damaged or discarded tender (not "tenter") poles acquired by us were treasures indeed, as, saturated by fish oil over many years, the whole pole ignited readily when a match was applied. These made excellent torches when the whole area was blotted out by the kippering smoke as we paraded through the village, waving them about.

If we had nothing better to do, my mates and I would meet after our tea and have a look at the kippering houses. My brother Roddy's was the nearest one, and, providing the large garage-like door was open, we would stand outside and gradually edge our way in.

The inside of the building seemed to be divided into three parts: the herring-slitting benches occupied one part, the kiln was the second part, and the unloading area the last part.

The kiln appeared to be a building within a building, and was totally divorced from the rest of the floor area. The only entry was through double doors which were usually left open until the fires were lit.

Apart from my brother, the smoker and his two mates, the building was empty, the girls had gone, the gutting-benches had been hosed down, and herring were not to be seen. We could see the smoker inside the kiln, crouched down by a pile of wood-chips on the floor, shaping them with his cupped hands and moving on to the next pile.

214

Similar attention was given to all twenty or thirty heaps, and when all were rounded up to his satisfaction, he would apply a lighted match to each heap. His mate, following him, held a metal sawdust-laden scoop over each fire and, gently tapping the scoop, sprinkled the sawdust over it until all flame was extinguished and only smoke was seen to come from the smouldering fire.

Occasionally the smoker would return to one of the fires and, on bended knees, would gently blow into the heap, in order to make it draw to his liking. As the emission of smoke increased, or if a flame were noticed, more sawdust was called for and tapped over the errant heap.

I could never see very much skill in this job — until I had the total process explained to me by a young lad, Tom Geddes, whose father was a smoker from Peterhead. The only interest Tom had in life was to become a kipper smoker like his father. "Ye see," he told me, "the fires have to give aff smoke for eight hours, and if a fire goes out it must not be relit, as this would mean the stour frae the auld fire going up the lum and sticking on to the kippers, and we couldna hae that, could we?

"The skill in kippering is being able to keep the puckle o' chips smouldering a' the time; to heat up and burn the sawdust, and then you have to add a puckle more.

"If you don't watch each of the fires and add on too much sawdust, the 'hert' o' the fire will gang oot, and then you would be in a bother. Now do you see?"

The next part of the process was turning the kippers; that meant changing over the position of the top racks with those on the bottom.

"Ye see, the nature o' the smoke has gone by the time it has driven through the stacks, and so the top ones widna be much guid."

Without any respiratory precautions the smoker and his mate would run, heavily laden, up and down the smoke-filled kiln with racks of kippers in each hand. How they managed to do this without having to hold on or to cough and splutter, I don't know, as the interior was filled with a dense cloud of acrid smoke.

On either side of the kiln door there were two acetylene lamps directed on to the now unoccupied unloading area. They gave off a very white light and lit up the total exposed floor area.

Sometimes it was possible for us to help refill the lamps with carbide chippings and, naturally, a fair share managed to fall into our pockets.

Great prestige was accorded us when we were able, at a later date, to drop the "chucky stones" into a pool and, with a lighted match, set the water alight, much to the amazement of the young audience.

The door to the kiln was usually kept shut, as too much draught would cause the fires inside to burn much too quickly, and only occasionally would the smoker or his mate have a "keek" inside to check on the fires.

Later in the evening the ubiquitous herring box was put into position to serve as the table, and similar boxes placed edgewise provided the seating accommodation.

The fags were produced, and a not unpleasant smell of tobacco pervaded the atmosphere.

Soon it was time for a bit of supper. The main item on the menu was always kippers and, if we were lucky, we were given one each. Each selected kipper of yesterday's smoking was rolled up in about ten layers of greaseproof paper and placed on one of the smoking-fires.

When ready it was taken to the table; the burned and charred paper was dumped on the floor, and there, inside, was a lovely golden kipper in pristine condition, ready for immediate consumption. At home we often had fried kippers for tea, but they were never as tasty as those eaten with our fingers in the kippering house.

Brother Roddy kept us well supplied at home, and the skin and bones were given to the hens, which resulted in the eggs tasting of kippers. I well recall my brother Duncan telling my mother that the hens were getting fed up with their diet, when she complained that the eggs were getting scarce.

I clearly remember our one and only frying pan. It was a great big black cast-iron affair, at least one foot in diameter, with a pail-like handle, which could be folded down out of the way, on top.

At any rate, when we had ham (the word "bacon" was unknown in our house) and eggs for our tea the predominant taste was kippers.

The pan was never washed, as I remember, and before use was put on top of the fire until the kipper grease liquefied. That was then poured away and the pan was given a good wipe with either the *Oban Times* or the *Daily Record*, whichever was to hand. This rendered it serviceable for further use, even for the making of stovies or pancakes, or the re-heating of last week's tattie scones — flavoured, of course.

The kilns were emptied in the morning and the kippers, eased off the still hot tenter hooks, were stacked on the gutting bench, ready to be packed by the girls.

The boxes for the kippers were made up from purpose-made wooden slats, and the older boys were employed for this part of the process.

How I envied them banging in the nails. I was unable to have a shot of this, and I would have been willing to do it all day for nothing, but as the older boys were paid for every container properly assembled, I was considered too wee, and pushed aside. The boxes from Roddy's building were marked in red stencil:

MALLAIG KIPPERS
RED M BRAND.

Kippers, like shoes, were sold only in pairs — half a box was 10 pairs, a box was 20 pairs. They were wrapped up in layers of greaseproof paper, and the filled boxes were piled up on the benches, awaiting transportation to the railway trucks. Most of the half boxes went to the post office and, at the cost of 6d., were sent to any nominated address and delivered by the postman in some far-off English town.

The last evening passenger train slipped into Mallaig at quarter to six. I say "slipped" as it always free-wheeled down from the hillside, to end up at sea level. My father was usually on this train, and its arrival heralded tea time. There was no need for clocks or watches, as I knew that when the train came in I had to run home if I was to get my tea.

Smoke everywhere

The kippering kilns, too, seemed to be conscious of this time arrangement, as very shortly afterwards the insidious kippering smoke appeared. In a very short time, thanks to twenty or so kilns competing in the smoke emission stakes, the pier area, and then the whole village, completely disappeared, blanked out with dense smoke.

Sometimes there would be a football match on Annie's Field (which I had helped to level) and at the end, about eight o'clock, going down the brae, we could see nothing — no lighthouse light, no houses and, of course, no sea.

Strangely, if it were a still night there was no sound at all, and all the smoke seemed to rise up to a common level, and instead of rising higher seemed only to become more dense, so that from the top of Annie's Brae you looked over a flat plateau with clear sky above. It didn't get dark until about ten o'clock during the kippering season.

With a little imagination we could have been sitting in a rowing boat on top of the water.

We youngsters enjoyed the dense smoke. I loved the smell; no trees grew in the area and the smell of

219

burning wood was quite unknown to us — scented slightly with kipper, it could not be excelled by the best Chanel perfume.

Another reason we enjoyed the smoke was that we were able to go places and do things normally forbidden under cover of the smoke screen. I was made nostalgically aware of this during my army days in World War II.

Another advantage the smoke had was that when it appeared, the midges disappeared. Speaking of midges reminds me of a conversation between Roguie and his relieving mate, in Roguie's signal box. The mate had apparently been accosted by a visitor who asked him: "What did the midges feed on before we came?"

In these conversations between shifts my ears were always cocked for the latest local tit-bits, two of which I will relate, though, puns being beyond me, I understood neither at the time:

Second signalman: The minister said all the fisher lasses coming to Mallaig were chased and should be respected as such.

Roguie: Chased, maybe, but they can't run very fast and are easily catched by the boys.

Second signalman: Aye, but do you not see this is their ploy to catch the boys and get married.

For myself I saw no boys chasing girls nor girls chasing boys at the pier, although I did go many times to have a look. The second tit-bit I think worth telling is this:

Roguie: Thae fisher lassies didna come tae Mallaig a' the way from Eyemouth or Burnmouth to gut the herring, you know.

Second signalman: Whit way, then?

Roguie: They came because they thought Mallaig was the Road to the Isles!

Second signalman: Oh aye, oh aye!

Even I thought this was very strange, as I knew that Mallaig was the terminus for the island boats, and surely those girls, having travelled almost the whole length of Scotland, must know this.

CHAPTER
THIRTY-ONE

The Khyber

I must have been about eleven or twelve when a group of huts appeared on the foreshore on the opposite side of the bay to the pier. As children we noticed this, but made little comment, assuming that these huts in some manner had to do with the fishing or were to house a further influx of fisherfolk.

Much later I heard from talk at home that the huts were to house workmen who were going to make a road round the top of the bay leading to an area commonly known as the Khyber. Well do I remember my mother being up in arms: "A road round the Khyber, whatever next?"

Our main road to Fort William extended only to the bottom of Annie's Brae and now we were going to have a new road, every bit as long, to go round the Khyber. The Khyber area was the original seat of the indigenous population and consisted of four or five crofts with some half-dozen detached houses, recently built. At present the only approach was by sea, or at slack tides by walking over the exposed stepping stones.

Roddy managed to get a job on the road-building; it might have been his first job, or perhaps the fishing was very poor. In any case I heard him saying that he was to be a knapper man. This was made real to me when he took his knapper hammer home. It was a very small hammer head mounted on a long, pliable shaft and was used to knock or chip stones into some sort of level order between the haunching stones which other men put into position to define the edge of the road. At home Roddy carried his hammer as though it were a rifle.

At school one day our teacher asked each of us where our parents and brothers and sisters worked. I said my brother worked on the new road round the Khyber and proudly intimated that he earned twenty-five shillings a week. When I told my mother she was furious. She would be at the school first thing in the morning and would sort out this new teacher, Miss MacLean. "What business of hers was it anyway?" Eventually my sisters, with a little help from my father, pleaded with her not to go and, knowing her temper, I was very sorry for myself and dearly wished I had not started this at all. Anyway, someone suggested that a letter to the headmaster was the best arrangement, but my mother's reluctant agreement necessitated an all-night sitting. I don't remember the final outcome, but it was a very serious matter and, of course, being the instigator, I was severely told off by my sisters, who had had their sleeping time curtailed — in addition, one of them had the unenviable duty of delivering the letter.

Some months later Roddy was able to tell my parents that new houses were to be built round the Khyber and that the road had been built just to transport the building materials. The house builders were to come from Glasgow and would take up occupancy of the huts when the road makers had finished. When it was finished it was a sand-covered affair with a surface coating of gravel and, while it looked very good, it was just not possible for us to ride our bikes on it as the wheels sank into the soft sand. I don't remember it ever being tarred. It didn't even go as far as the last croft but stopped just short of Prince Charlie's Cave.

Prince Charlie's Cave

Every village from Glenfinnan to Mallaig had a cave, or at least some house, where Prince Charlie was reputed to have stayed or hidden, and every MacDonald (and there were a lot of them) was related to Flora MacDonald, famed as his escort and means of his successful escape to Skye en route to France.

Our cave did, however, have an occupant, one who was neither kith nor kin to the Young Pretender. I saw him several times and to me he looked a very old man, complete with bushy beard. It was said in the village that he had been a bank manager who had become a recluse and forsaken all modern conveniences and the company of others.

I believe he was an educated person and I do know that he walked daily to the village to collect his requirements from the shop but, more importantly, he would visit the station and collect his daily paper. It was either the *Scotsman* or the *Glasgow Herald* or perhaps both, and I imagine he had had to have them specially ordered at John Menzies' book stall. I know very little more about him but he bothered no-one and, like Mr Wolfe, was generally accepted and perhaps even respected. Later I learned his name was MacAulay, which to me was suggestive of Irish origin.

Blasting

When the Khyber road was finished and pronounced passable, preparations for house building were put in hand. It seemed to me that the whole hillside had to be blasted away in order to make provision for the level foundations. At school all lessons were stopped as the noise of the blasting and the rattling of windows rendered any conversation impossible.

A new boy arrived in my class; he lived in one of the Khyber huts with his father who was a shot firer. He told us that when the holes had been drilled into the rock face he helped his father tamp in the black powder while his father added the detonator and prepared the fuse.

It is clear that he was well-versed in explosives as he told me that the fuses had each to be exactly six inches longer than the previous one. The reason for this was, firstly, that each explosion was counted by his father and the number had to tally exactly with the total number set and, secondly, it gave time to go from each fuse in turn, as the time needed depended on the distance between the fuses. We told him we didn't believe him, but one day he made his point and frightened us to death when he came to school with a length of fuse. To us it looked like a length of rope, but when he lit the end and the flame spluttered along the "rope" we ran for our lives. He stood quite undaunted and assured us it was perfectly safe but that once the fuse had been lit it could not be put out, even if put in a bucket of water. The only way to stop it burning was to cut it. I was greatly impressed by his knowledge.

It was said locally that the blasting was necessary to make room for the foundations, and that, coupled with the need for making the track in which to run the fresh water supply in and the pipe to take the sewage out beyond the low tide mark, meant that the blasting cost almost as much as each building.

House Building

Two tenements were eventually built, each with accommodation for twelve families, four to each floor. I say "eventually" as the crofters resented this intrusion into their peaceful environment. I remember hearing that all the timber for the buildings had disappeared and, although the local policeman was called in, no trace was ever found. Replacement timber arrived some time later but even this was removed and found floating in the bay or washed up on the shore; in any case very little was recovered.

Floating wreckage was governed by maritime rather than civil law. Any wreckage is considered to be flotsam (accidentally washed overboard) or jetsam (deliberately abandoned in an effort to save a ship in distress or to

226

diminish the likelihood of loss of life). The only exception was in respect of wreckage on which duty had to be paid. This was the responsibility of the Coast Guard, who had the power to solicit the aid of the police and have the wreckage impounded. Seaborne wreckage was never reported to have arrived at Mallaig. All flotsam remains the property of the owner and although the timber fell into this category, by the time the matter had been sorted out all the timber had drifted back out to sea, and of course was never reported to have ended up at Mallaig.

Interior fittings of the new tenements, like sinks, baths and toilet pans, too, had been spirited away, and it was said in our house that the old sink used as a flower-tub in front of the police station house had been supplanted by a new unit.

CHAPTER
THIRTY-TWO

Leaving School . . . and Mallaig

When I was about twelve or thirteen I was able to find a part-time job as a message-boy with the largest grocer's shop in the village. This was operated by Willie MacLean, Davy's brother (the brae is still called Davy's Brae).

There were three grocers' shops in the village, and when a fishing-boat tied up at the pier it was the custom for a shop assistant to jump aboard, hoping to get an order for groceries; if our shop was successful I was required to help with the delivery. My duties included delivering messages to houses around the village, but this was the best part of the job, particularly as a proper bicycle was provided, complete with rectangular carrier in front, housing a wicker basket. I don't remember getting paid for this job, but it was common to be given a tip, and the joy of riding the bike made payment superfluous.

Well do I remember one of my tips. I had some provisions to deliver to Mrs Campbell, who lived a little way beyond the village. I had often done this and it was

228

usual for her to give me two Abernethy biscuits; this day she told me she had run out of these, but would I, instead, take two cream biscuits? I was delighted with this, and patiently waited while she went "ben the hoose". I waited expectantly, as I knew about cream biscuits, which had only just come on the market. Shortly before, Cathie and I had shared a packet of MacFarlane Lang's custard creams. She had managed to "borrow" the grocery book, and I was sent to the shop. Between us we gobbled up the lot in one go. Imagine my joy of anticipation as I heard Mrs Campbell returning — she gave me two Jacob's cream crackers! Of course I thanked her and put them in my pocket for the hens.

My fourteenth birthday was in August and I didn't go back to school after the summer holidays. Instead, I continued with my messenger boy's duties, pretending to my mother that I was still attending school; she even made up my playtime piece for me, and as the days, and even the weeks went by, I consoled myself that when I was caught out (as I knew I would be one day) the penalty would diminish in proportion to the lapse in time. How wrong could I be!

My mother arrived at the shop and I was marched through the village by my mother, berating me at the top of her voice. Arriving home, I was made to strip off and she washed me from head to toe before laying out my Sunday clothes. We were off to the school.

My mother was also dressed in her Sunday best: a navy-blue coat, blue hat complete with flower in the hat band, and of course, round her neck she wore her fox fur. This fur showed a beautiful fox's head with two bright glass eyes which looked so real that I often used to stare at them, hoping that they would blink. My mother, with her tall, regal figure, looked quite formidable and as, in any case, a parent coming to school was a real rarity, the whole of the Junior School waited patiently to see the outcome.

My mother *demanded* to see the Headmaster, and when told he was taking a class, said she would go and get him out. One of the teachers said we were to go into the Staffroom. This was the Holy of Holies, and if I had had any doubts before, I now realised the seriousness of it — I was in the Staffroom! The Headmaster arrived, very red in the face and obviously very angry, my mother was furious, and I was terrorised. Mother was rather subtle in her approach and asked (very kindly, I thought) if he would have me back at school. The Headmaster was adamant: no. Education was compulsory for all children until the age of fourteen. "Your child has attained this age, and consequently we have fulfilled our duty towards him." Mother tried once more to have me reinstated, but to no avail; she was told that further education was not possible, and in any case I had had my chance at the Qualifying Exam, where I recorded the lowest score ever in Mallaig school: 3 marks out of 100. In addition, I had always been a disruptive influence and had always set a poor example to the younger children.

Mother was speechless. She went through the usual routine: never any trouble at home, always did his homework, loved coming to school. She was sure that I was a little immature and that one more year at school would be to everyone's advantage, but to no avail. NO MORE EDUCATION. We left the Staffroom and marched through a crowd of children playing in the yard. The playing stopped when we arrived and we passed on in silence.

All the way home Mother nagged on, only quiet as she aimed many a good skelp at me, which I, in turn, made every effort to avoid, but unsuccessfully most of the time. Her chant was, "You made me look a fool," and "Wait till your father comes home, I'll see he takes the belt to you."

The belt was my father's razor strop and, while I'm sure it was pressed into its subsidiary duty, I have no specific recall of the incident, although knowing my mother, I'm sure it did take place. It was a fairly commonplace situation and I think my father must have dreaded his homecoming, wondering what misdemeanour of mine he was to hear about. Suitable punishment had to be meted out before he had his tea, and this could be about nine o'clock as the preamble normally took at least an hour and the discussion of my misdeeds continued even after my parents were in bed.

After the novelty of not attending school had worn off, I realised that I couldn't stay as a messenger boy for the rest of my life. My choices were very limited: I couldn't get a job on the railway because of my eyesight, and this left only the fishing. I had no wish to become a member of a boat crew, and in any case I don't remember ever seeing a fisherman wearing glasses. I didn't want to job like Roddy, wandering from

231

one fishing village to the next in pursuit of the herring, like an Arab nomad. I was really concerned needlessly, as it happened. Fate took a hand in my future, and shortly after my fifteenth birthday my father "got a shift" to Crianlarich, while I ended up, after several false starts in local part-time jobs, as an apprentice in Edinburgh.